WATER GARDENING

for Everyone

by Philip Swindells

First published in 1996
by Burall Floraprint Limited, Wisbech, UK

Copyright © Burall Floraprint Limited, 1996

A CIP catalogue record for this book is available from the British Library

ISBN 0 903001 72 1

Floraprint books are
by Burall Floraprint Limited, Wisbech, UK

Philip Swindells began his horticultural career as a student at the University Botanic Garden, Cambridge. This was followed by a period working at the famous water plant nursery of Perry's of Enfield. Various management positions followed culminating in the curatorship of Harlow Carr Gardens in Harrogate. Since 1990 he has managed his own horticultural consultancy and worked on water garden projects in as far flung places as Spain and the Middle East. He contributes regularly to the national gardening press and is a frequent broadcaster on local radio and television.

Picture Credits
All photographs are from the Floraprint collection with
the following exceptions:
Anglo Aquarium Plant Company Ltd,
pages 58, 59, 60, 61

Typeset by Dolphin Graphics
Illustrations by Christine Sampson

Printed in Singapore

Contents

An Introduction to Water Gardening

The place of water in the garden

Although water gardening has in recent years achieved widespread popularity through the introduction of modern materials for pool construction, it has been an important feature of gardens from time immemorial. Over three thousand years ago waterlily ponds were recorded as being the principal feature of the famous palace gardens of Ikhnaton. The Greeks in Homeric times constructed nymphaeums with constantly running water and the Japanese dug pools in the shapes of birds and animals in which they grew all kinds of water plants. Ancient Chinese gardens also featured pools, alive with decorative carp and framed with rushes, while the Indians held waterlilies in high regard and they were widely acclaimed by the great literary minds of the day.

It was probably the high regard which man always had for waterlilies that induced him to cultivate them, and so start a primitive form of water gardening. Certainly the ancient Egyptians must have used large quantities of waterlily blossoms.

Their monarchs were often laid to rest with wreaths made from the petals of the tropical blue-flowered *Nymphaea caerulea*. These were placed on the mummy in regular patterns until the sarcophagus was full of floral tributes. The reason for this custom was the belief that the beautiful blooms of the waterlily rising pure and clean from the slimy mud were comparable with purity and immortality. The two principal aspirations of man.

Waterlily blossoms were used in other religious festivals and also offered to visitors as a gesture of friendship and goodwill. So they were obviously quite important to the people of that time who were evidently skilled water gardeners.

In Britain we do not have such a long association with water gardening, although the native white waterlily, *Nymphaea alba*, has long been cultivated and its rootstock harvested for the making of dye. The earliest reference to water gardening in this country was made in 1731 by Philip Miller in his famous gardening dictionary. He writes, 'In some gardens I have seen plants cultivated in large troughs of water, where they flourish very well and annually produce great quantities of flowers.'

Water had, of course, been used extensively for its own sake. Purely as a mirror or to break up the landscape. However, the serious business of cultivating and developing aquatic plants did not take place until Paxton, and a little later Marliac, started introducing and hybridising aquatic plants, more particularly waterlilies. Even if it has not always taken quite the same form, man has had a long and enduring relationship with water gardening, an alliance that is being continually strengthened with the passage of time.

This passion for water is not difficult to understand, for it is a creature of many moods. Sometimes a raging fury, occasionally a lyrical whisper, but more often a placid mirror. It is because it can be so varied that it has such a widespread appeal. The young identify with the bubbling frothing fury of a mountain stream. Then with the embrace of first love they forsake it for the romantic, soft, swaying curtain of droplets from a gentle fountain. While those of us mellowing with the years delight in the cool glassy stillness of a pool which quietly reflects all about it.

Choosing a site for a pool

There are several things to consider when planning a water garden. Not just practical points to take into account, but aesthetic considerations which in the end will have an overwhelming influence upon the success of the venture.

Certainly time and thought given to selecting a site is not wasted, for unlike many other garden features, a pool once constructed is not easily moved.

In order to come to the correct conclusion we should heed the words of Alexander Pope. 'To swell the terrace, or to sink the grot; in all, let Nature never be forgot'. Seldom is water discovered naturally above the lowest level of the ground. Only when trapped will it remain in such a position, looking distinctly ill at ease and impatiently waiting to cascade down to lower reaches. Only in a formal garden, where the pool is contained within a raised walled surround, does water rest in peace.

In an informal setting water has to be at the lowest level in order to be in conformity with its surroundings. Unfortunately, this is not always the best position from the gardener's point of view, for such a situation may be beneath over-hanging trees or in the shade of a high wall. When such a problem presents itself, the only way it can be overcome is by skilfully planting the garden to create the illusion that the pool is in fact in a natural situation. Excavated material from the con-struction can be used to raise the surrounding ground level and will do much to assist in this trickery.

Ideally, a pool should be sheltered from cold easterly and northerly winds by a fence or low wall. Or if an integral part of a rock garden, then should preferably be constructed to the south or west of protective rocky outcrops. It is surprising how much effect even modest protection from cold winter winds will have upon the degree of freezing within the pool. Any reduction in icing and increase in protection for emerging plant growth in early spring is most welcome.

The limits imposed by aesthetic considerations can present practical problems. These are not normally insurmountable, but the aspiring pool owner should be aware of them at the outset. Aquatic plants, for instance, require full uninterrupted sunlight if they are to prosper. Such conditions encourage prolific growth which is essential both in maintaining a balance within the pool as well as providing much appreciated surface shade for the fish. Pools constructed in the shade are invariably gloomy and are difficult to establish a balanced collection of plants in. They are, therefore, almost always anaerobic and evil smelling.

Close proximity to deciduous shrubs can bring trouble. In the autumn blowing leaves are likely to accumulate in the water unless care is taken to cover the pool with a net. If a pool has to be built in such a situation this precaution should not be disregarded, for decaying vegetation in the water generates toxic gases which can be lethal to the fish. Especially if the pool becomes covered with ice during the winter and these gases have no means of escaping into the air.

Not only can the foliage of decaying deciduous species be harmful, but evergreens like holly and laurel have leaves which are extremely toxic to fish. So are the seeds of the lovely spring-flowering laburnum. These contain a readily soluble alkaloid which will very quickly poison fish.

Other trees, particularly those of a weeping nature which are normally associated with water, must not be allowed to overhang the garden pool. That is the pool should not be constructed in the proximity of an established tree nor at a later date should any such tree be planted nearby. The reasons for this are many, not least of all the problems likely to be encountered with strong probing roots disturbing the pool foundations.

Apart from this, and the normal problems associated with pool contamination from falling leaves and other debris, there is the question of inspect pest control. Many tree species harbour the over-wintering stage of troublesome pests. Of these, the waterlily aphis is of the greatest concern to the water gardener. This causes extensive disfigurement of aquatic plants and spends the winter on the boughs of flowering cherry and plum trees. Of course some measure of control can be effected during the winter by spraying the trees with tar oil winter

Skilful planning creates the illusion that the pool is in a natural situation.

wash. However, this task is impossible in the case of a weeping cherry which overhangs a pool, a situation to be avoided at all costs.

A final, and often overlooked, consideration is the provision of electricity. Certainly if moving water or artificial lighting are contemplated this must be close at hand.

Formality and informality

Not only is the position a pool occupies in the garden important from a technical and visual point of view, but it should be such that it easily blends in with the surroundings. A circular or rectangular pool usually looks completely out of place in an old cottage garden, while the tangled informality of an irregular pool does not associate well with a broad sweeping lawn and neatly clipped hedge.

As in any other aspect of decorative gardening one has to have an overall policy of formality or informality. It does not follow that one style has to be enforced throughout the garden for both formal and informal areas can be created, separated by a hedge, border or trellis. Formal water gardens tend to be reflective, and if carefully placed can give quite remarkable illusions of space. The informal kinds are constructed more for the pleasure of cultivating a variety of aquatics, although they are still an important part of the overall garden scene.

Personally I prefer the informal kind as I am particularly interested in the plants and other aquatic life. But I would concede that a formal pool can be extremely rewarding and that its quiet stillness is more mentally soothing than the busy tangle of an informal pool. From a practical point of view it is certainly much easier to manage.

The question of formality and informality really only affects the surface design of the pool and the visible materials with which it is constructed. It does not matter whether the pool is made from a pool liner, concrete, or fibreglass, but the way in which it is finished is of paramount importance. A formal pool should be finished neatly with paving or a coping, while an informal one can be incorporated at the base of a rock garden or the edges disguised with creeping plants or turf.

A formal pool must be designed with straight lines, even curves, or it can be circular or oval. The important thing to remember is that it should be balanced, and that any fountain or ornament that is to be added, placed in such a position that when viewed from any angle the effect is one of equilibrium. The same applies to a certain extent with plants, although perfectly balanced planting does not always have the desired effect. A strategically placed clump of rushes in one corner of the pool can often have a dramatic effect which could not be equalled by planting a clump in each corner. Indeed, planting a formal pool successfully is not quite as easy as one might imagine for it is not a case of the more plants the merrier. It is more a question of obtaining a visual balance between plants and water so that the reflective qualities are retained. But not at the expense of the plants, for these are essential in maintaining a natural balance and provide continued interest for the gardener. Again Alexander Pope puts into words what our intentions should be, in a far more eloquent manner than I could ever achieve. 'But treat the goddess like a modest fair, nor overdress, nor leave her wholly bare.'

Informal water gardening is more easy going. To my mind there are two types of this kind of gardening. The first is generally displeasing to the eye and I will only mention it here as a warning to the prospective pool owner. This is the plantsman's pool in which the enthusiast grows as many different varieties of plants as he can in tangled profusion. It usually looks messy to anyone but the owner, who is so totally engrossed in the intricacies of the plants that he never stands back and sees the pool for what it is. I have a certain sympathy with him, for once you get hooked on water plants it is difficult to stop collecting and growing them. But a collection should be retained in tubs or tanks away from the decorative garden. Certainly nothing looks worse than a dozen or more individual marginal plants spaced equidistantly around the edge of the pool, together with a clutter of waterlilies which almost totally obscure the water surface.

Proper informal water gardening is a careful blending of what pleases the eye and the plants which the owner has grown to love. These can be planted in an irregular fashion, but in bold groups to make a good effect. The pool itself should merge with the surrounding garden, whether it be lawn, rockery, or bog, and plants from both within and around the pool be encouraged to mingle.

A common misconception amongst informal water gardeners is that the surface of the pool should be bristling with deep water aquatics and the broad verdant pads of waterlilies. This is not so, for an over-planted pool which obscures much of the water surface loses a lot of its appeal. Even in an informal setting reflections and water movements are very important.

Apart from over-planting, the other trap that the pool owner may fall into is what I call fussiness. This is the designing of a pool with all kinds of niches and contortions which seems to be aimed at proving

The careful selection and correct positioning of plants contribute to the success of this formal pool.

What has happened in such an instance is the same that occurs in a stream. Water meets an obstacle such as a projecting rock which causes a deviation in its course. Invariably where it comes into contact with such a promontory it is thrown against the opposite bank and an extended recess is the result. Thus an informal pool will always have a more pleasing appearance if the boldest promontory is almost opposite the largest recess in the opposite bank. It is also important to note that the pond edge seldom finishes abruptly and usually forms a slope which continues below water level. This is not always easy to contrive, but where it can be achieved the effect is quite remarkable.

The use of moving water

There can be few more beautiful sounds than the gentle whispering of water over rocks or the tinkling of fine spray from a fountain as it falls into the pool below. Indeed, moving water is often the prime reason for introducing a pool into the garden. For it is only water that can be used to give movement and life to a garden setting without appearing totally artificial. Of course the ways in which it can be utilised are legion, but before making any suggestions we ought to become acquainted with the practical side of providing a fountain or waterfall.

Electric pumps are widely used and these are available in two types. The submersible pump, which is placed on the floor of the pool and recirculates the water, and the larger kind which recirculates the water in the same way, but must be installed in a waterproof chamber towards one side of the pool. The latter is only used for moving large volumes of water and will be of little use to the average pool owner, although it is as well that he is aware of its existence.

that this is what informality is all about. Unfortunately such excesses are not pleasing to the eye and are often difficult to maintain. It is far better to have gentle sweeping curves with definite radii. Indeed, to construct an informal pool successfully and obtain the best effect it is prudent to observe nature.

As intimated earlier natural ponds are usually found at the lowest level in the landscape. When these have evolved as a collecting basin for drainage water from the surrounding ground, they take on a rounded or oval appearance. These dewponds often accommodate an abundance of aquatic plant life which throngs the margins and slowly advances into deeper water. Although we can learn a certain amount about the manner in which plants are naturally found and distribute themselves, this particular kind of natural pool is not the best on which to base one's observations. Except to reaffirm that water is invariably found at the lowest level and is always better observed from above.

The ideal natural pond type to study in order to create a really good effect is that which has at some time been evolved from an expanded stream. The edge or 'shoreline' of such a pool has been made by the action of water and produces exactly the right appearance for the decorative garden.

The submersible pumps are generally the most satisfactory, for they can be used to operate either a fountain or waterfall, or both simultaneously, and are available in a range of capacities that will satisfy most pool owners. They are surprisingly compact units and consist of an inlet, which has a strainer to extract debris, together with the motor and a narrow outlet which can be attached to a variety of accessories. Either a single outlet with a narrow hose which can be used for a waterfall, a series of fountain jets to create different spray patterns, or a two-way outlet which will accommodate both.

Moving water can be used in many ways, but care should be exercised when designing a pool to see that it does not interfere with the plants. Waterlilies, and indeed the majority of decorative aquatics are inhabitants of quiet backwaters and dislike moving or turbulent water. Not only that, but waterlilies will not tolerate the continual spray from a fountain on either flowers or foliage. The leaves turn black and rot, while the blossoms ball up and then fail to open.

If we take a look at fountains, we discover that there is little that can be done with them other than alter the height or spray pattern. Not unless we go on to something really adventurous. One splendid arrangement I have seen uses a fountain and a series of bowls. Water is pumped up a tall central stem and then tumbles into a small bowl. Beneath this are strategically placed bowls of similar structure but gradually increasing sizes. On filling the first bowl, the water falls into the one below and the process is repeated until it reaches the pool. As the bowls are level in a horizontal plane, water falls evenly around their rims creating a delicate watery curtain which captures sunbeams and explodes them into a twisting kaleidoscope of colour.

The main problem with an ambitious project such as this is the excessive turbulence created in the pool below. This makes life intolerable for most aquatic plants, although some measure of success can be achieved by arresting the undesirable movement within a large ring placed immediately beneath the fountain. Water plants can then be encouraged to grow in the relatively peaceful outer perimeter.

Apart from straightforward fountains, gargoyles, masks and ornaments can be used to spray water. They are usually imitation lead or stone and depict animals, children or faces. The larger free-standing ornaments are useful in a formal setting. They often depict a lion or perhaps a water-nymph and can be stood beside the pool and allowed to spray water back in. This gives the gardener the opportunity of having moving water without unduly interfering with his plants, for turbulence is restricted to a small area quite close to the edge.

Gargoyles or masks depicting all manner of natural and mythical faces serve a similar purpose and are very useful in small gardens. As they are intended to be fastened to a wall the gardener with limited space need only construct a semi-circular pool against the wall for the water to spout into. He can then enjoy the pleasure of moving water, still grow a few aquatics, and keep fish in half

The negative effects on plant and fish life, of turbulent water, can be minimised by restricting the area affected to one edge of the pond.

An Introduction to Water Gardening

the space his restricted circumstances might otherwise have dictated.

Another variation on the fountain which can be used successfully in a small garden or courtyard is what I call the pebble fountain. This involves no plants, just moving water. To make one of these a small concrete chamber must be constructed to hold a reasonable amount of water and a submersible pump. A framework of iron rods is laid across the top which supports fine mesh wire netting. On top of this a generous layer of well-washed pebbles is placed and the outlet from the pump drawn up until it is at the surface of the stones. Water then bubbles up and through the pebbles creating a cool, refreshing effect. The only thing to remember is that with such a feature evaporation is rapid and therefore the chamber beneath will need constantly replenishing with water.

The grotto is one step further on from this, and although not to everyone's taste, can provide a focal point in an otherwise dull and uninteresting corner. A pool is constructed with a background built up along the lines of a rock garden. A small, natural-looking cavern is constructed at the summit and contains a pump outlet surrounded

by liberal quantities of well-washed pebbles. These stones extend down a water-course over which the constantly recirculated water tumbles. When tastefully planted with ferns and other moisture-loving subjects the whole feature takes on a quiet dignified air comparable with that of an empty church with high vaulted ceilings.

This sort of atmosphere cannot be said to exist with ordinary waterfalls, for most of the pre-fabricated units produced by plastics manufacturers today are of unnatural shape, colour and texture. But they are essential if your waterfall is going to be successful. Primarily because they will contain and direct the water without having any adverse effect upon the surrounding ground. Any attempt at constructing a natural rock waterfall will lead to disaster. Not only will it look unnatural, but all kinds of debris from the surrounding ground will be washed into the pool and pollute it. A good strong cascade unit is vital, but please disguise it as much as possible with rocks, pebbles and moisture-loving plants, for nothing looks worse than a stark blue fibreglass cascade unit fed by a bright green hose.

Gardeners with a little more enterprise can construct another

form of waterfall called the water staircase. Many years ago this was not infrequently encountered in French and Italian gardens. Of course, in most cases it was a spectacular feature demanding large quantities of water. But in the garden it can be scaled down so that the flow from a submersible pump in the pool below is sufficient to make it effective.

The idea behind the feature is to make a staircase which appears to be constantly moving with the flow of water. This can be achieved in the garden by the use of sizable concrete drainpipes set in a bed of concrete one behind, and slightly above, the other. Thereby making a staircase with rounded steps. The hollow ends of the pipes are filled with concrete or suitably disguised with soil and plants. However, if the pipes are new and have not been weathered give them a treatment of sealer to ensure that the harmful free-lime in the cement is not washed into the pool below. Ordinary glazed pipes serve as well, but although harmless look most unnatural.

The outlet hose is then taken to a small pool at the summit of the staircase and the water allowed to cascade down.

Underwater lighting

Perhaps it is because we spend so little time in the garden during the evening owing to our irrational climate, that we seldom consider installing artificial lighting. Pools, waterfalls and more particularly fountains, can be made breathtakingly beautiful by the use of strategically placed lights. These are available in a multitude of colours and are quite safe if used sensibly and the manufacturer's instructions are followed.

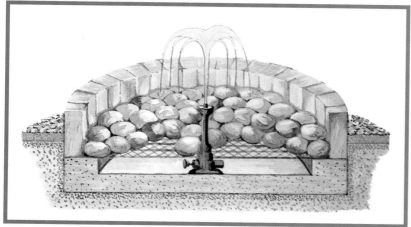

A pebble fountain

Constructing a Water Garden

The essential features of a garden pool

Before buying or building a garden pool, it is essential to be aware of the requirements of future inhabitants. Waterlilies and other deep water aquatics require specially allocated positions in deep areas of the pool if they are to flourish, while marginal plants, such as reeds or rushes, are grown on a shallow shelf which extends around at least part of the edge.

Waterlilies will grow in widely varying depths of water according to their variety, some living happily in as little as 15cm of water, while others will tolerate in excess of a metre. Most of the popular kinds, however, grow best in 45cm of water and when a prefabricated pool is contemplated it is essential to see that such a depth is available together with ample level space on which to stand the planting containers.

Marginal plants occupy the shallows towards the edge of the pool. These should be about 20cm deep and sufficiently wide to accommodate a planting basket. Many prefabricated pools are made with very narrow, shallow shelves on which the plants are intended to be planted directly into soil or compost. But for reasons which I will explain later this is an undesirable practice.

Having made provisions for the plants we should not overlook the requirements of the ornamental fish. Fancy goldfish, such as telescopes and fantails, need a depth of at least 45cm of water if they are to over-winter successfully. But ordinary goldfish and carp will usually survive quite happily in a minimum depth of 20cm.

As with all other garden features one must plan well ahead. Decide as clearly as possible which plants and fish are to be accommodated and then purchase or construct a pool with their well-being in mind. A reversal of this procedure leads to endless trouble.

There is one other point that must be considered and which varies from one garden to another. This is pool size. It is impossible to say that a particular pool is suitable for one garden, for gardens, pools, and personal tastes are very different. But a pool that is either too small or too large for its surroundings is a blot on the landscape.

To get some idea of the size and shape necessary to give the desired effect, take a length of hosepipe or rope and form the outline of the pool on the site. This can be adjusted until one is satisfied. Measurements can then be taken and the method of construction decided upon.

Making a pool from a liner

Pool liners are one of the most popular forms of construction for they are relatively inexpensive and can be used to create any shape that the gardener desires. They are quite simply a large sheet of rubber or polythene material which is placed in an excavation the size and shape of the finished pool. The liner is installed and secured to the edge of the pool by rocks and paving slabs. Water is added and the liner can then be moulded to the contours of the pool.

There are many different kinds of pool liner in a widely varying price range. So many in fact, that the newcomer to water gardening is likely to be confused and make a costly mistake unless he studies all the sales literature very carefully.

Liners of 500 gauge polythene in a sky-blue colour and three or four standard sizes are the cheapest. These are intended for selling in quantity at the lower end of the market. While not condemning them completely, I feel that they have little to offer the serious pool owner as they are liable to have a very short life.

Deterioration is most marked

between soil and water level. If exposed to the rays of the sun the polythene bleaches, becomes brittle, and then cracks. Furthermore, some aquatic plants can puncture a polythene liner with their spear-like creeping root stocks, reed maces (*Typha latifolia*) and bur reeds (*Sparganium ramosum*) being particularly adept at this.

The manufacturers of this type of liner claim that it will last up to ten years. While this is possible with extreme care, the more usual life span is three or four years. So bear this in mind when being tempted by its lower price. Where it can be ideal, is for providing a quick and cheaply constructed sanctuary for ailing fish, a nursery for young aquatic plants, or somewhere to put the fish and plants when the pool is being cleaned out.

Polythene liners should not be confused with those made of similar, but more robust, polyvinylchloride (PVC) material. These are economical and durable liners which represent excellent value for the beginner. There is an even tougher version incorporating a terylene web to give the liner extra strength.

Low density polythene (LDPE) liners appear to be even more resilient. These have a much greater burst resistance and are as close as you can get to the durability of rubber.

However, it is rubber which is the most resilient material for pool lining. It is virtually indestructible and has been tested over many years in commercial applications. Sunlight and frost seem to have little effect upon its black matt finish, and the only way in which it can be punctured is by accidentally sticking a garden fork through it. They can be coloured using special non-toxic paints. Certainly any gardener seriously considering a permanent water garden would be well advised

to consider using this material.

To calculate the size of liner required, first measure the length and width of the intended pool. Or if it is to be an irregular shape, the size of the rectangle which will enclose the entire shape. Then measure the depth of the pool and the width of the anchorage. Add these figures to both the length and width, to arrive at the overall size required.

Irrespective of the material used, lining a pool follows along broadly

the same lines. The excavation is scoured for any sharp object like flints and sticks which may damage the liner. A layer of builders' sand is then spread over the pool floor to act as a cushion. If the soil is rough or stony then thick wads of dampened newspaper can be used to line the walls to prevent any projections from ruining the liner. Alternatively purchase protective fleece which is manufactured specifically as a protective underlay. It is theoretically ideal, but in

As with all other garden features, plan well ahead to achieve the desired effect.

practice quite difficult to install without creating undulations beneath the liner.

The excavation is then ready. If the liner is the polythene variety, it should be spread out in the sun for an hour or so in order to become pliable and easier to work with. Unsightly wrinkles often occur with polythene and these should be dealt with as the level rises. They are impossible to straighten out once the pool is full.

A slightly different technique must be adopted for PVC, LDPE and rubber liners. These are more flexible and can be stretched out evenly across the excavation using bricks or paving slabs to hold them in place. Water is slowly added and as the liner tightens the anchoring weights are slowly released until the pool is full and the liner pressed to the outline of the excavation. When full, any surplus material can be trimmed, but about 30cm allowed to remain for securing with paving slabs or rocks. Once the edge is neatly finished, the pool can be planted, for none of the specially manufactured pool liners contain anything that is toxic to plants or livestock.

Before departing from pool liners I should mention that they are invaluable for making a bog garden. There must of course be an allowance in the calculations for the extra material necessary.

The idea is to construct the bog garden adjacent to the pool by making another shallow excavation like a huge marginal shelf. This should be of the order of 30cm deep. The pool liner is then used to line the excavation and the shallow bog area in one piece. A barrier of stones or bricks can then be placed across the division between pool and bog. This will retain the soil in the bog garden and yet allow the water to seep through. It is essential when refilling the bog area that the level

Digging out the pool.

Finishing the sides. Avoid making them any steeper than 45°.

The plastic liner is carefully spread out.

Constructing a Water Garden

of soil is well above that of the water, or else it will just become an extension of the marginal shelf.

However, it seems that if moisture-loving plants are sitting permanently in saturated conditions they will not prosper. This can be overcome by providing a 6cm layer of coarse gravel on the floor of the bog. Then a mixture of peat and soil is added as the growing medium. The gravel then acts as drainage and a reservoir. If the plants can grow with their collars above the water and yet dangle their roots into it they seem blissfully happy.

Installing a preformed pool

Preformed pools are very popular and durable, although they are probably the most expensive. They are made of two kinds of material; plastic and fibreglass. The plastic ones occupy the cheaper end of the range and are vacuum moulded in a tough, yet lightweight material. These are either grey, green or blue and often have a simulated rock finish. For the newcomer to water gardening they are ideal, being light and easy to handle. The only complaint I have about them is their design. With few exceptions they only make scant accommodation for marginal plants.

The same applies to the majority of fibreglass pools. Which is regrettable as they represent an excellent investment for the serious pool owner. Again they are available in a wide variety of shapes, sizes, and colours. However, beware of the smaller kinds referred to in catalogues as rock pools. These are intended to be placed at the summit of a rock garden and act as the supply vessel for a cascade unit. They hold very little water and are generally unsuitable for any aquatic life.

Fountain trays are a similar proposition. Being very shallow they

During the filling, the pool forms itself.

End of May to Mid-June is ideal planting time.

are incapable of supporting any aquatic life. Their intended role is as a pool for the water constantly recirculating through a fountain, or from a gargoyle affixed to a wall.

Installing a preformed pool is not difficult if one knows how to approach the job properly. But it is fraught with difficulties for the uninitiated. Most manufacturers recommend that a hole is dug to the size and shape of the pool. In practice this is virtually impossible. So what must be done is invert the pool in the position in which it is to be installed and mark out a rectangle that will enclose all the most distant points. It does not matter that the pool is inverted and therefore the surface shape is reversed, for the rectangle that is transcribed will be exactly the same size. It is just that it is easier to accurately assess the overall size of the rectangle this way.

The hole should be made as deep as the greatest depth of the pool and the floor levelled up with a layer of sand. The pool is now placed in position and supported on bricks so that it is at the desired level. It should be level from side to side and end to end, yet 3-4cm below the surrounding soil level. Careful levelling ensures that water does not flood out of one end and leave the other dry, while placing the pool slightly below the finished ground level allows for its inevitable rise as the hole is backfilled and rammed firm.

The importance of levelling cannot be over-emphasised, and the use of straight boards on which the spirit level can be rested will ensure accuracy. As the pool is slightly below the level of the surrounding ground to begin with, a short board will be required to level the width and a longer one for the length. These being used continuously during the backfilling process.

If the excavated soil is coarse and stony it should not be used for backfilling as problems with air pockets and subsidence might occur. I always prefer to use sand, filling the hole evenly and gradually removing the supporting bricks. If the sand is rammed tightly around the pool it will provide ample support.

Pool construction in concrete

A well-made concrete pool will last for years and is a constant source of pleasure. Unfortunately one sees many badly constructed concrete pools and these cause endless heartaches for their owners. What annoys me most about these pools is that they have one common and easily avoidable fault – haste in construction. For some inexplicable reason a man building a pool in concrete almost always loses his patience. He is so keen to get it finished and the plants and livestock introduced, that he skimps on essential tasks. But it is attention to detail that makes the difference between failure and success.

A design should be chosen that does not have walls that are too steep, nor curves and niches that are fussy, as these are difficult to build in concrete. Once a plan has been formulated the hole should be dug so

that it is 15cm larger all round than the finished size. Any loose or crumbly soil must be firmed and the excavation lined with heavy gauge builders' polythene in the same manner as one would use a pool liner.

When concreting a pool it is better to finish the job in one day so that all the concrete unites rather than over a period of several days, for leaks will often appear at the various unions. If it is impossible to complete the job in one day, be sure that the edge to be joined is roughed up so that the next day's mix keys with it. No more than twenty-four hours should pass between the last mix and the first one of the next batch if leaks are to be avoided.

Mixing concrete is a wearisome task, but contrary to popular belief, there is nothing mysterious about it. A satisfactory mixture consists of one part cement, two parts sand, and four parts gravel, measured by volume either in a bucket or on a shovel. This is then mixed with a shovel in its dry condition until of a uniform grey colour. If one wants to play safe and introduce a waterproofing compound it is done

at this stage, but stick to the manufacturers' instructions.

Water is gradually added to the mixture which is constantly turned until of such a consistency that when a shovel is placed in the mixture and withdrawn with a series of jerks, the ridges formed by the movements retain their character. Concrete in this condition is ideal for laying. A mixture that is too wet often produces air bubbles and hair cracks in the surface, while a dryer agglomeration tends to crumble.

Well-mixed concrete is spread evenly over the pool floor to a depth of 10cm and as far up the sides as possible. Wire netting is then spread out over the surface of the concrete to act as reinforcing. The final 5cm of concrete is then laid over the top. The surface is finished with the deft sweep of a plasterer's trowel.

When the sides of the pool are very steep or vertical some kind of formwork will have to be erected. This is usually made of rough timber and held in position to make a mould for the walls. Unfortunately concrete will stick to wood, so it is essential to limewash, grease or soak the boards with water before the

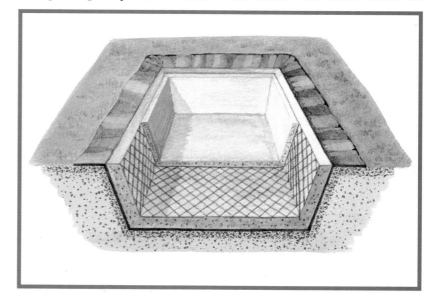

The construction of a concrete pool.

concrete is poured in. This will ensure a neat clean finish when the formwork is removed. If the design is a little more irregular and the harsh straight lines of boards are not desired, plywood can be used. Being supple and bending to almost any shape it is extremely versatile, but remember that concrete can exert quite a pressure and any plywood or hardboard shuttering contemplated would have to be generously reinforced with stout timbers.

Coloured concrete can be made by adding pigments. These should be mixed with cement in any proportion up to 10 per cent by weight. Red iron oxide gives a red colouring, chromium oxide a rich deep green, cobalt blue a pale blue and manganese black a black, while the use of snowcrete cement and fine Derbyshire spar yields an excellent white finish.

Once the concrete has been laid and any remaining surface water soaked away, all exposed areas of the concrete should be covered with wet sacks. This is particularly important during hot weather, for if the concrete is allowed to dry out too quickly hair cracks will appear. If a large area of concrete is involved, frequent spraying with water from a watering can with a fine rose attachment will have much the same effect. This treatment is only necessary for a couple of days. Within a week the concrete will have set and we can then consider stocking the pool.

This is not possible straight away, for unlike liners and prefabricated pools, concrete structures contain a substantial amount of free-lime which can be harmful in varying degrees to both fish and plant life. One only needs to look at the milky water in a freshly constructed pool to see just how much of this harmful substance is present.

The harsh concrete backdrop is softened and disguised by cascading plants.

The patient gardener can leave the pool unstocked and open to the weather. After six months the concrete will be mature and relatively harmless. However, most of us having completed the hard physical work would like to see some progress made with planting. For us there are several alternatives.

Emptying and refilling the pool a number of times has the same effect upon the concrete as being exposed to the weather. But this is a laborious business and it is difficult to be certain when it is safe to introduce life. By far the best way of dealing with the free-lime problem is by using a neutralising agent.

I still like to fill the pool once and then empty it so that all the grit and similar debris is washed away. Once it has dried out the neutralising agent can be applied. It is usually sold as a white powder which, when mixed with water, turns into thick paste. Application is by brush, being sure to cover the entire surface. Apart from neutralising the lime, it reacts with

the concrete and forms silica, thus sealing the concrete by internal glazing.

Another way of curing concrete is by using ordinary household vinegar. One part vinegar to 200 parts of water by volume. Allow this solution to remain in the pool for three days and then empty and rinse thoroughly. The pool will then be safe.

This can be done much quicker using 1 part vinegar to 10 parts water and scrubbing the concrete with a stiff brush. I am a bit hesitant about doing this as the concrete often bubbles and becomes rough with the chemical reaction. If you should decide to do it this way be sure to wash the pool out before introducing plants and fish.

Rubber and liquid plastic paints are often used to waterproof or safely alter the colour of a concrete pool. They are available in a number of pastel shades and once applied form a thick rubbery skin over the surface of the concrete. In doing this they not only prevent water from seeping away, but do not allow free-lime to escape. Most of the paints sold for this purpose react with the concrete and do not form a smooth waterproof skin unless it has been treated with a suitable primer.

Sometimes it may be found necessary to repair a concrete pool. This creates all kinds of problems, not least of all providing alternative accommodation for the plants and fish. It is, of course, necessary to remove them all, for if any freshly mixed concrete pollutes the water it can create all kinds of trouble.

When a leak is located, the cracked or crumbling area should be chiselled out until solid concrete surrounds it. The cavity can then be filled with the usual concrete mixture and allowed to set. A rubber or liquid plastic paint is then used to seal it completely. No guarantee can be given as to the permanency of such a repair, but under most circumstances it is satisfactory.

When either sealing a new concrete pool, or repairing an established one, most, if not all, of the water has to be removed. It was the fashion with pools which were built during our grandparents' time to have a drainage system with a plug of some kind in the floor. This created a weakness and often resulted in the break-up of the pool at that point. As most pools were situated at the lowest level in the garden this made the task of constructing a satisfactory drain and soak-away quite difficult.

Certainly a drain cannot be recommended for a concrete pool and is impossible to incorporate in a pre-formed or lined construction. Apart from baling out the water with a bucket, which is perfectly acceptable when dealing with a very small pool, the ideal method is to attach a length of hose to the submersible pump outlet. Providing the pump is not required to lift the water any higher than the fountain or waterfall it normally operates, the hose may be of any length necessary to safely transport the water to a more distant part of the garden. Obviously, every last drop will not be removed, but the 15 or 20cm that remain can be baled out with a bucket and any residue removed with a mop.

When a raised formal pool needs to be emptied this can be quite simply done by siphoning the water off with a length of hose. Providing that the outlet is always lower than the level within the pool, the water will flow continuously.

The use of tubs and other containers

It is important to realise that water gardening need not necessarily be confined to the garden pool. Even those who are restricted to a modest courtyard can enjoy the wonders of aquatic life by utilising various containers.

Tubs are the obvious choice for a miniature water garden venture. Those made for shrubs being particularly useful. However, more often than not they are made from old barrels that have been sawn in half and then made watertight. These may have contained all kinds of substances, many of which could cause problems. Old wine and vinegar casks or beer barrels are fine, but beware of those that have contained fats, oils, tar or wood preservative. These are extremely difficult to get clean and leave an unsightly and often toxic scum on the water.

Second-hand sinks make excellent water gardens, but being rather shallow are not really suitable for goldfish. One or two tiny fellows that are brought in for the winter will keep down any mosquito larvae. But sinks should always be watched carefully during hot weather as such a small volume of water heats up quickly and soon causes the fish to gasp.

It is not my intention here to make specific planting suggestions, for it is obvious that dwarf aquatic plants and pygmy waterlilies are well suited to this kind of enterprise. However, there is one other avenue open that is beyond the scope of this book, and that is the cultivation of tender aquatics which can be over-wintered indoors. Many of the most spectacular, like the tropical waterlilies and sacred lotus, become dormant during the winter and their rootstocks can be easily stored in damp sand. If treated in much the same way as bedding plants they can create quite spectacular effects. With the need for annual soil replacement and the difficulty of over-wintering some hardy subjects in such confined spaces it provides an excellent opportunity to experiment with these gorgeous tropical aquatics.

Natural water gardening

Gardeners with a natural pool are fortunate indeed. For water that has accumulated naturally and found its own level is invariably pleasing to the eye. Slight alterations can be made to suit one's purpose, but generally the only improvements are those that come with skilful planting. Of course, with modern trends in housing and gardens we are less likely to come across a natural pond. However, there are those who abhor anything artificial and crave to construct a pool that is as natural as possible.

Before the introduction of plastics, polythene and fibreglass, pools were often made of puddled clay. Although not the most successful of structures, the technique by which they were built is worth relating.

The excavation having been

The careful distribution of excavated soil has enabled this raised pool to be successfully established in a potentially unnatural situation.

Constructing a Water Garden

completed, the walls and floor were dampened and then given a liberal coating of soot. This was a deterrent to worms who delighted in puncturing the clay finish. Very wet clay was then daubed like plaster over the entire pool surface, care being taken during construction to ensure that as work progressed the clay that had been puddled was kept damp. Occasionally spraying with water from a watering can with a fine rose attachment usually did the trick, although on large expanses a covering of wet hessian sacks was a much less laborious method of preventing drying.

Once completed, water was quickly run in and care taken to see that the finished level of the puddled clay coincided with the water surface. If any gap between ground and water level was exposed to the sun the clay would shrink and fall away. Thus on very warm days, even with an established pool, a hosepipe had to be kept at the ready to replace the water lost through evaporation.

As intimated earlier, this is an outmoded method of construction, but worth relating if only to acquaint the reader with the problems involved. Books and articles often recommend it as an economical way of building a pool. It may be economical in cash, but it is certainly not in time.

Those who prefer a natural-looking pool will be interested in a soil sealant method of construction which has been in use in the United States for several years. Although the product itself is not yet freely available here, it does seem to present a useful alternative method and is worth looking out for in the future.

The sealant is an emulsified polymer which causes soil particles to bond together. It does not work on very sandy or stony soils, nor those that are exclusively peat. However, on loams, clays and those in between, it provides a simple method of reducing seepage by up to 95 per cent.

The pool is dug to the finished size and the soil packed as tight as possible with the back of a spade. Water is added until the pool is about half full. The sealant is then introduced and thoroughly mixed with the water. As more water is added stirring is continued to ensure thorough distribution.

It is important that the pool is kept full to the top during the sealing process. This will take twelve to twenty days. Any drop in the level of the water at this time will result in the exposed area not being sealed properly. During this process the water is milky and extremely toxic to fish. It takes three or four weeks to clear and become safe, but it is as well to test it first with one or two inexpensive goldfish.

Drying-out can cause problems with this kind of pool after sealing. Fortunately this can be alleviated by the use of a floating valve attached to an inlet pipe which will allow just sufficient water to enter. This could, of course, also be fitted to a puddled clay pool where the drying problem is more acute.

Few ideas that seem so simple and successful have no drawbacks at all and the soil sealant is no exception. Manufacturers recommend that algaecides and other chemical pond treatments should not be used as these can break down the seal. I also wonder what happens when the probing roots of aquatic plants ramify the walls or floor. These will surely cause seepage. The whole technique is relatively new to us in Britain and we should perhaps not criticise it until we have gained more experience. It has certainly been used commercially for the construction of man-made lakes and lagoons in the United States for a number of years.

Gardeners with a natural pond are fortunate indeed.

Planting a Pool

Creating a natural balance

Creating and maintaining a balance within the pool is the most important aspect of water gardening. Sadly, it is the one that is least understood. One needs no specialised scientific knowledge before bringing about a satisfactory natural balance. Common sense is the prior requirement, together with the application of a rough and ready formula which in a fairly short space of time will produce the desired result.

One should regard a pool as a miniature underwater world. In this it will be seen that livestock, such a fish and snails, deplete the water of oxygen. Yet the gaseous and organic products yielded by this livestock are necessary to maintain plant life. During their natural processes plants release oxygen, the submerged ones obviously doing so in the water and thus providing a lifeline for the fish and snails.

Unfortunately, natural balance is not quite so easy as this, although the cycle just described is an essential part of it. Water that is rich in mineral salts and exposed to full sunlight soon becomes alive with algae. These are primitive plant forms and vary from the filamentous kinds, like blanketweed and silkweed, to the suspended varieties that create a green bloom or pea soup-like effect in the water. The coarser filamentous kinds invade and choke desirable aquatics, while the suspended varieties obscure light from submerged plants and retard their growth. Although technically plants, their presence in quantity does little to ensure fresh healthy water.

To create a balance in which their presence is negligible and the water bright and clear, it is necessary to assess our armoury. Obviously by reducing the amount of light falling directly into the water, algal growth will be reduced. To ensure that this does not hamper the submerged oxygenating plants as well, no more, but not much less than one-third of the surface area should be covered by foliage. Floating plants can provide much of this, although it must be realised that waterlilies can contribute significantly with their floating pads.

The battle beneath the surface is fought by the submerged plants. Being more advanced forms of plant life, they compete with the primitive algae for mineral salts in the water. If present in sufficient numbers they starve the algae out and thereby ensure clear water. A generous bunch of plants to every 0.093 square metres of water surface area ensuring reasonable success from the beginning.

Of course, creating a correct balance by planting the various components in sufficient numbers does not ensure clear water and harmony from the start. Remember that algae, being primitive forms of plant life, grow and reproduce rapidly. Therefore, they will invade a pool quickly and only be reduced gradually as the intended pool plants become established. The period of time that this takes varies considerably, but may be as little as four weeks or as long as ten weeks. If green or unhealthy conditions persist beyond this time, then the balance cannot be in order and the cause must be investigated. Even if correct at the beginning, plant deaths can have a significant effect upon the balance, and replacements should be made as and when necessary.

Planting in containers

In my view aquatic plants are best grown in containers. Not that they do any better, but they are certainly easier to manage. If the pool needs cleaning out they are easy to remove. Likewise, when the plants need lifting and dividing they can be swiftly dealt with. Container cultivation also restricts one variety

Aquatic planting baskets.

to its allotted space. A free-for-all amongst aquatic plants leads to an almighty tangle that is very difficult to care for and results in the ultimate demise of weaker and often more desirable plants.

Pots are sometimes recommended for aquatic plant culture, but these are generally unsuitable on two counts. First of all they are of the wrong shape, having too narrow a base, taller plants like irises and rushes continually toppling over. The more important point is that a number of water plants, notably waterlilies, quickly diminish in size if grown in a container that does not have lattice-work sides to allow the free passage of their roots. There would appear to be no scientific explanation for this, and therefore, one can only speculate, but it is a practical fact that many aquatic plants are stunted by normal pot culture.

Proper aquatic planting baskets are now made of plastic and are either round or square with open-work sides and broad bases to ensure stability. Occasionally it is possible to get old-fashioned wooden planting crates and these are equally suitable, if less durable.

If one picks up a gardening book written at the beginning of the century, when water gardening, as we know it, was in its infancy, it will be noted that all kinds of concoctions are recommended for the culture of water plants. Old rotted cow dung was a particular favourite for waterlilies, together with turf and decayed leaves. Fortunately, we have now dis-covered that all these old formulas are unnecessary and in many cases can be harmful.

The introduction of rotted manure and turf to a garden pool creates almost instant green water, for the mineral salts liberated as it absorbs the water are legion. If perchance the manure was not in such a state of decomposition as recommended, it could itself pollute the water and kill the fish. As we will see later, we now do all we can to prevent leaves falling into the pool and creating problems, rather than deliberately introducing them in the compost.

A suitable compost for all aquatic plants consists of garden soil from which all the debris like sticks, leaves, and pieces of turf has been removed. It should not have been collected from a part of the garden that has been recently dressed with artificial fertiliser, for, like organic matter, this also encourages an algal bloom. Under no circumstances should soil be removed from wet, low-lying areas as this often contains the seeds of pernicious water weeds which may be difficult to remove later.

Having cleaned the soil up and run it through a sieve to remove any large stones, a little fertiliser can be added. This must be of a slow release kind like bonemeal or hoof and horn. It should be used sparingly and in as coarse a grade as possible. The finely powdered form quickly clouds the water and can be toxic to fish.

Before planting, the prepared soil should be dampened to such a consistency that when squeezed in the hand it binds together, yet is not so wet that water oozes between the fingers.

Planting aquatics differs very little from planting ordinary garden plants. Firmness, and positioning at the correct level in the soil being of the utmost importance. Slight variations of technique do apply to certain waterlilies and all submerged oxygenating subjects.

Hardy waterlilies have two different modes of growth. Those derived from *Nymphaea odorata* and *N.tuberosa* producing horizontal rhizomes, while the marliacea, laydekeri, and intermediate varieties usually grow from bulky, log-like rootstocks with fibrous roots arranged like a ruff around each crown. These are planted vertically or at a slight angle with the crown just above the compost.

Before planting a waterlily remove all the old adult foliage. This will eventually decompose anyway and in the meantime will give buoyancy to the plant and may even lift it out of the basket. Fibrous roots should be trimmed back to the rhizome and any dead or decayed tissue cut back to sound healthy growth. Exposed areas of sound tissue should be dusted with powdered charcoal to reduce the risk of infection and help seal the wound. If a rhizome looks somewhat gelatinous and has an objectionable smell, destroy it immediately. This is almost certainly the highly infectious waterlily root rot.

Marginal subjects are planted in the same manner as one might any other container or pot grown plant. However, submerged oxygenating plants are treated differently. These are usually sold as bunches of unrooted cuttings fastened together near the base with a strip of lead. Although seeming to be clinging precariously to life, once introduced to the pool they rapidly initiate roots and grow away strongly.

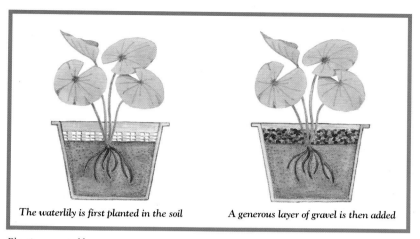

The waterlily is first planted in the soil

A generous layer of gravel is then added

Planting a waterlily.

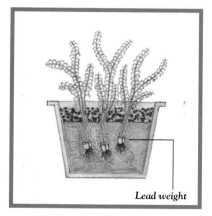

Lead weight

Submerged oxygenating plants should be planted so that the lead weights are buried.

They do not rely entirely upon nutrients supplied by the compost and can indeed exist for a considerable length of time just floating about in the water. But rooting gives them stability. The important point to remember when planting the bunches, whether into a container or directly into soil on the pool floor, is to bury the lead weight. If exposed to the water it quickly rots through the stems and the top of the plant falls away.

When all the containers are planted, firm the compost down and add a layer of pea gravel over the surface. This prevents fish from nosing in the soil and stirring it up. At the same time it traps any organic debris in the soil mixture which may float about in the water. The baskets can then be given a thorough soaking with water from a watering can in order to settle the compost and drive out all the air.

Planting the natural way

For gardeners who have a natural water garden, or those who desire to plant directly into the pool, a slightly different technique has to be adopted. Gardeners with an artificial pool are, in my opinion, ill-advised to use direct planting methods for the reasons I outlined earlier in the section on planting in containers. Certainly plants growing in containers are easier to manage and keep within bounds.

The only advice I can offer to those to those who insist upon direct planting, is to be sure to have a substantial depth of soil, at least 15cm, for the plants to root into. Also cover the entire surface of the soil mixture with pea gravel to prevent the fish from stirring it up.

In a natural pool one has no option but to plant into the floor and banks. Making a hole and pushing the plant into the margin is seldom successful with reeds, rushes and the like. I like to get a plant which has been pot grown and with a decent rootball, for this has stability and grows away much more quickly.

Waterlilies can be placed directly into the pool in a plastic basket or wooden crate. But a more tidy approach is to parcel them up in a square of hessian with a good helping of compost and lower them into position. The hessian eventually rots, but in the meantime the waterlily roots will push through and ramify the soil on the pool floor. Submerged oxygenating plants can be merely tossed in. The lead weight pulling them down into the mulm. Some will come adrift as the lead rots through the stems, but most will take root.

Planting a new pool

When planting a new pool it is possible to position waterlilies, other deep water aquatics, and submerged plants on the pool floor before adding water. But be sure that waterlilies, in particular, are placed in an open, sunny position away from the turbulence created by a fountain or waterfall. Also ensure that the foliage of both deep water subjects and submerged oxygenating plants is wrapped in polythene to prevent it drying out while the pool is being filled.

Some gardeners favour the running in of enough water to cover the foliage of plants which are occupying the pool floor. Raising the level as the leaf stems on the waterlilies extend. This is all very well, but if marginal plants are being installed at the same time they are left high and dry and in constant need of watering. By far the best idea is to raise the waterlily baskets on bricks so that the crown is just beneath the final water level. As the leaf stems extend the bricks can be removed until the basket is at the required depth.

When direct planting in a pool with soil spread over the floor, it is impossible to deal with waterlilies in this way. Under such circumstances refrain from introducing marginal plants until all the deep water subjects are established. Marginal plants have very little bearing upon the balance of the pool and their temporary omission allows the pool to be filled slowly as the waterlily foliage grows. Of course, if this is not possible the waterlily can be planted directly into the deep area, but will take a lot longer to become established.

When filling a pool, especially one with a soil-covered floor, there is usually trouble from muddy water. It follows that if a hosepipe is just placed in the pool it will inevitably stir up the compost and distribute it in a cloud around the pool. To prevent this happening place the end of the hosepipe on a sizable sheet of polythene allowing the water to trickle over the edge. As the pool fills, the water level rises lifting the polythene sheet and hosepipe. The polythene is trapped

between the water surface and the end of the hosepipe, but is easily removed once the pool is at the desired level.

Planting in an established pool

Occasionally, replacement plants will be required in a well-established pool. Planting of these differs very little from those that are intended for a new venture. The same baskets, soil mixture, and preparation going into replacement stock as when the pool was initially established. This may seem to be stating the obvious, but it is a sad fact that many gardeners neglect to make such a good job of planting additional or replacement plants.

Another important point to heed is plant health. The introduction of diseased stock can lead to considerable damage, particularly if infected with a highly contagious disease like waterlily root rot. Snail eggs should also be

removed, especially those in long cylinders of jelly which belong to the troublesome freshwater whelk. I would also make a point here that native aquatic plant life should not be introduced, especially directly from the wild. Apart from unforgivably reducing our natural flora, such plants may be infested with fish parasites and be host to leeches, scorpions and other horrors of the deep.

The actual placing of plants in the water follows along the lines described earlier. Waterlilies and other choice deep water aquatics being raised on brick pedestals and gradually lowered as they grow. Some pool owners lower the baskets on strings and hooks, but these are not often satisfactory. To make a proper job of it place a strong board across the pool on which to kneel and then roll your sleeves up.

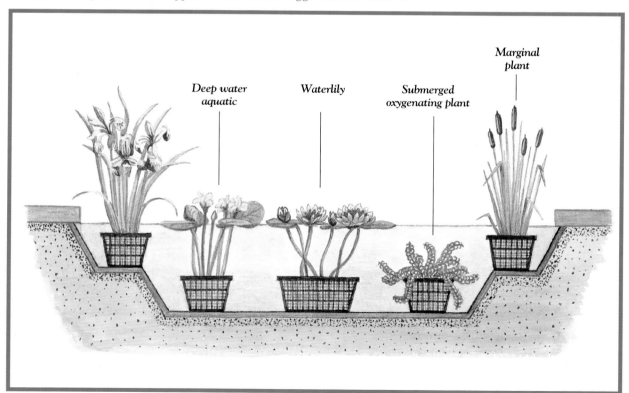

Deep water aquatic   Waterlily   Submerged oxygenating plant   Marginal plant

A well planted pool.

Waterlilies and other Deep Water Aquatics

The waterlily – queen of the pool
The waterlily, 'How stainless it rises from its slimy bed. How modestly it reposes on the clear pool, an emblem of purity and truth. Symmetrically perfect, its subtle perfume is wafted far and wide; while there it rests in spotless state, something to be regarded reverently from a distance, and not to be profaned by familiar approach'. Thus wrote the eleventh century Chinese author Chou Tun-I in an eloquent passage which describes so perfectly this magnificent aquatic. Yet the waterlilies grown at that time were fairly ordinary white and yellow species. One, therefore, speculates as to what he would write if he could see the wealth of colour and diversity of form available to the modern gardener.

There are now hardy varieties that are suitable for growing in anything from an old kitchen sink to a lake, and in double, semi-double and single-flowered forms in every colour except blue. However, as there are a number of blue-flowered tropical species it is probably only a matter of time before this colour too is infused into hardy stock. Foliage is from light green to bronze, plain or speckled. It may be the diameter of a small coin or the size of a dinner plate. The variation amongst waterlilies is unending and gives immense scope to the skilful planter.

Several varieties provide excellent cut flowers, particularly those derived from the North American species *Nymphaea odorata*. Some flower arrangers float the cut blossoms on a bowl of water, while others make an attractive arrangement with cut foliage inserted into a floral wire holder which is totally submerged. Unfortunately, most waterlily blooms close on the evening of the first day that they are cut and never re-open. This can be remedied by standing the freshly cut blossoms in iced water for an hour or so. Such a severe shock prevents them from ever closing again. Alternatively, a spot of melted candle wax can be dropped at the base of the petals where they meet the stamens. This forms an unobtrusive wedge which prevents the flower from closing.

Selecting suitable varieties
Waterlilies are known botanically as nymphaeas, although plants as diverse as our native *Nuphar lutea* (yellow pond lily) and the giant tropical *Victoria amazonica* are referred to as waterlilies too. Probably the most familiar true waterlily is our native white *Nymphaea alba*, a vigorous plant with large, fresh green leaves and snow-white, cup-shaped blossoms. It is much too vigorous for the garden pool, requiring in excess of a metre of water in order to do itself justice, and occupying a vast amount of surface area. However, together with its red form *N. alba rubra* it has proved invaluable as a parent of many modern hybrids.

Nymphaea odorata has played an equally important role in hybridising, but it is also an excellent garden plant in its own right. Being of modest proportions and growing in as little as 45cm of water it is one of the finest scented waterlilies for the garden pool. Its individual blossoms may be 15cm or more across and are borne amongst handsome, fresh green foliage. A soft pink form, *N. odorata rosea* (Cape Cod waterlily), is exquisite and *N. odorata rubra* startles all with its vivid crimson blooms.

Nymphaea odorata has been hybridised variously with other species and its own sports to yield a distinctive race of cultivars of similar habit and with the same rich fragrance. All of these are easy-going, thriving in about 50cm of water. Except for 'Helen Fowler', a more vigorous kind with immense, richly scented, deep rose blossoms up to 25cm across. This variety requires slightly deeper conditions, but still produces tidy clumps of pale green foliage.

'Luciana' is of similar colour but more modest growth, while 'William B. Shaw' is creamy-pink with deep red internal zoning. 'Firecrest' has sparkling pink blossoms with conspicuous red-tipped stamens. Its foliage is purplish, and except for the lack of mottling, of a similar hue to that of the popular canary-yellow-flowered 'Sulphurea'. But my favourite amongst the odorata hybrids is the bright rose-pink 'Suavissima' with its rich cloying fragrance.

For the very small pool the diminutive *N.odorata minor* (mill pond lily) can be recommended. A native of the shallow bogs of New Jersey, this little beauty has sweetly scented, white, star-like blossoms 8cm across and tiny, soft green leaves with dark red undersides. Another closely allied miniature, *N.odorata pumila*, produces similar blossoms, but has dark green leaves with a purplish cast.

Nymphaea tuberosa (magnolia waterlily) is another North American native but of more substantial proportions. The wild species is vigorous, with distinctive fleshy tubers which give rise to large, green, orbicular leaves and pure white, scentless blossoms. It is rather large for the modern water garden, but its cultivar 'Richardsonii' is of more tidy growth with splendid, pure white, globular flowers. Generally speaking the *N.tuberosa* varieties should be avoided by the home gardener and enjoyed in the pools of parks and public gardens where they have ample space to develop properly. However, *N.tuberosa* often produces improved seedlings and many of these have been selected, named, and become established and widely planted garden varieties.

Indeed, one of the finest,

Nymphaea 'Firecrest'

fragrant, pink-flowered varieties, *N.caroliniana*, is believed to be the result of a union between *N.odorata rosea* and *N.tuberosa*. Unlike its parents though, it is of modest growth and will flourish in as little as 35cm of water. A white form called 'Nivea' is equally agreeable, so too are the beautifully formed pale and deep rose-pink varieties 'Perfecta' and 'Rosea'.

The tough and resilient *N.candida* requires similar conditions and although not perhaps as elegant as *N.caroliniana* and its varieties, is nevertheless a valuable addition to the smaller pool. Particularly in colder areas. Many geographical forms exist, but these are only of interest to botanists. The typical plant grown by the nurseryman has white, scentless, cup-shaped flowers with golden stamens and crimson stigmas borne continuously from

Waterlilies and other Deep Water Aquatics

May until September.

Nymphaea tetragona (pygmy white waterlily) is equally floriferous, producing tiny, white, star-like flowers amongst small, dark green leaves that have rich purplish undersides. The flowers are complete miniature replicas of the larger hybrids, being sweetly scented and seldom more than 3cm across. As one might suppose this is really a plant for the sink or tub garden, although it can be used to good effect in a rock pool or planted towards the edge of a more substantial water garden. *Nymphaea pygmaea alba* is the plant usually offered by nurseries and garden centres and is doubtless just a form of *N.tetragona* improved by selection and cultivation.

Nymphaea tetragona 'Johann Pring' is a mutant which occurred in the Missouri Botanical Gardens. This has deep pink flowers up to 6cm across with distinctive rings of orange and pink stamens. Its leaves are dark green, like miniature lily pads, and provide a perfect foil for the delicate starry blossoms.

The pygmaea hybrids are of similar character and need shallow water too. Their parentage has been lost in the mists of time, but most gardeners acknowledge that they are probably the results of various crosses between *N.tetragona* and the half-hardy Mexican *N.flava*. All are free flowering and welcome additions to the garden pool Particularly the lovely *N.pygmaea* 'Helvola' with its beautiful canary-yellow blossoms, for this will come into flower only a matter of weeks after planting and is probably the best-natured waterlily of all. Unlike the other pygmy kinds its foliage has a heavy chocolate mottling, but this in no way detracts from the beauty of the flowers.

Nymphaea pygmaea 'Rubra' is the best of the miniature reds, sporting

Nymphaea tuberosa 'Richardsonii'

Nymphaea 'Maurice Laydecker'

Waterlilies and other Deep Water Aquatics

tiny stellate blossoms with vivid orange stamens amongst handsome, purplish-green leaves. The closely allied N.pygmaea 'Rubis' is larger in every part, while the old variety 'Hyperion' has blooms of the deepest amaranth. 'Maurice Laydeker' is sometimes sold as a miniature and although it does produce superb blossoms of deep vinous red, it is scarcely a pygmy and quite a shy bloomer.

None of the pygmy kinds will grow in more than 30cm of water. Most prefer less than half of that whilst the popular large flowering hybrids really need a depth of 60cm. Fortunately the void between can be filled by the group of waterlilies known as the laydekeri hybrids. These were developed by the famous French waterlily hybridist Joseph Bory Latour Marliac and named in honour of his son-in-law Maurice Laydeker. Their exact parentage is unknown, but all produce a profusion of medium-sized blossoms amongst compact groups of dark green lily pads.

Nymphaea laydekeri 'Purata' is the best known and most widely cultivated, a handsome plant with rich vinous-red flowers sporting conspicuous bunches of bright orange stamens. The bright crimson *N.laydekeri* 'Fulgens' is a worthy companion and *N.laydekeri* 'Lilacea' provides a notable contrast with its fragrant, soft pink flowers, while the sparkling white *N.laydekeri* 'Alba' has an aroma akin to that of a freshly opened packet of tea.

Nymphaea 'Moorei' is a more moderate grower. Its bright yellow blossoms and handsome mid-green leaves have a distinctive purplish spotting.

A similar group of waterlilies occurs within the popular range of more vigorous varieties and these are known as the marliacea hybrids. Once again these are of indiscern-

Water lilies seem synonymous with tranquility.

Nymphaea 'René Gérard'

foliage. On past performance it has earned itself a reputation for being invasive, but this is of little account in the garden pool where excessive growth is easily removed.

About ten species of elodea are known to be in cultivation, but only *E.canadensis* is widely grown. The plant frequently offered by nurserymen as *E.crispa* is not, strictly speaking, an elodea at all, but *Lagarosiphon major*. This is the plant frequently sold by the pet trade for goldfish bowls. A dark green, crispy-leafed oxygenator with densely clothed stems that look almost snake-like in the water. Like *E.canadensis* this can grow vigorously in conditions to its liking, but is easily controlled and actually benefits from an occasional severe pruning of over-exuberant growths.

Potomogetons are generally of more modest proportions, or, at least, those that can be recommended for the garden pool are. Never to be tempted to introduce species with floating leaves like *Potomogeton natans* and *P.lucens,* for although extremely decorative when young, they rapidly outgrow their positions in a small pool. The only species that can be unreservedly recommended are the small-growing, totally submerged kinds like *P.crispus* (curled pondweed) and *P.acutifolius* (sharp-leafed pondweed). The former is particularly desirable, for it has handsome, bronze-green, translucent leaves with crinkled and serrated margins, although *P.acutifolius* should not be neglected as it shares these virtues, but with leaves that are flat and entire.

Milfoils have delicate filigree foliage arranged on long, spire-like stems. These often terminate in tiny flower spikes which stand just clear of the water. Two species are popularly grown, *Myriophyllum spicatum* and *M.verticillatum.* Both

Eichhornia crassipes, a summer inhabitant of the pool.

look superficially alike, except that the leaves of *M.spicatum* have a distinctive pinkish cast, whereas *M.verticillatum* is a clear bright green. For the goldfish fancier these two are indispensable, their delicate, feathery foliage being an ideal site for the deposition of spawn.

The callitriches are equally valuable to the fish keeper. Their bright green, succulent, cress-like foliage providing the palatable green material so necessary for a balanced diet. Many species and forms find their way into garden ponds, but only *Callitriche platycarpa* (syn. *C.verna*) and *C.hermaphroditica* (syn.

C.autumnalis) are offered by nurserymen. These look very similar, except that *C.platycarpa* produces rosettes of narrowly elliptical floating leaves and dies down for the winter, while *C.hermaphroditica* is totally submerged but evergreen.

So is *Eleocharis acicularis* (hair grass) a real gem for the tub or sink-garden. A close relative of the sedges, it produces spreading carpets of slender wiry foliage, which, once established, looks just like seedling grass. It seldom grows more than 8cm high and does not interfere with other plants nor become infested with algae. Unlike most other submerged aquatic plants, eleocharis does not lend itself to bunching and is, therefore, sold as tiny rooted clumps.

Decorative submerged aquatics

Ranunculus aquatilis (water crowfoot) is one of the finest submerged aquatics for floral and foliar effects. It flowers during mid-summer with tiny glistening chalices of gold and white amongst deeply lobed, dark green, floating leaves. Its submerged foliage is finely dissected, somewhat flaccid, and of a paler hue. It grows in dense spreading masses and is useful in both still and moving water.

Hottonia palustris (water violet) must have calm clear water if it is to thrive. With handsome whorls of pale green, much divided foliage and spikes of delicate lilac or white blossoms it is a constant source of delight. *H.inflata* is of similar habit, but has strange flower stems that are grotesquely inflated. Both have the same pattern of growth as ceratophyllum, being strongly rooted during spring and early summer, but breaking up and retreating into turions which fall to the bottom of the pool for the winter months.

Floating aquatics

Floating aquatic plants are useful additions to the pool, not only being decorative, but reducing the amount of direct sunlight falling into the water, thereby making life difficult for water-discolouring algae. Like submerged aquatics they are capable of absorbing plant foods directly from the water thus providing stiff competition for the more primitive slimes and algae.

Floating plants can be loosely divided into carpeting kinds and individual free-floating varieties. The carpeting species, like the bright green native duckweed which infests ditches, ponds and waterways is familiar to all. One need not, therefore, stress the dangers inherent in introducing such species to our garden ponds, even though the enthusiastic fish keeper would doubtless defend their inclusion as being useful for providing green food for the fish. Only *Lemna trisulca* (ivy-leafed duckweed) is worthy of a place in the ornamental garden, for this has attractive, dark green, crispy foliage of well-restrained growth. It produces minute, greenish flowers of little significance.

The azollas have no flowers at all as they are really aquatic ferns. Two species are commonly cultivated, *Azolla caroliniana* and *A.filiculoides*. Both are so similar that only a trained eye can separate them. Indeed, in many cases the species are sold mixed together and as they are both as hardy as one another, their correct identities would seem to be of little consequence.

Both form thick mats of lacy, bluish-green foliage which, in bright sunshine and at the approach of autumn, take on rich crimson tints. As winter starts to bite, the handsome congested fronds become brittle and decompose. However, warm spring sunshine revives the over-wintering bodies which start into growth again towards the end of May. This is often rather late in the season to be effective against algae, so I like to keep a handful growing throughout the winter months. A jam jar of water with a little soil in the bottom which is stood on the kitchen window-sill will provide an advanced battalion to put out on the pool towards the end of April.

Similar precautions should be taken with *Hydrocharis morsus-ranae* (frogbit), for this retreats into tiny turions for the winter and is very slow to break into growth the following spring. Hydrocharis is a

Hydrocharis morsus-ranae, a charming native plant for the tub or sink garden.

charming plant with rosettes of small kidney-shaped leaves and attractive, white, three-petalled blossoms. These are produced regularly throughout the summer, and together with its modest habit, make this a most desirable acquisition for the tub or sink garden.

Stratiotes aloides (water soldier) is a close relative of the frogbit, although it really looks nothing at all like it. Only the flowers bear any resemblance. Delicate creamy-white blossoms, which on the male plant are borne in clusters in a pinkish papery spathe, and singly in the axils of the leaves on female specimens. Both sexes are of the same general aspect, looking very much like floating pineapple tops with their stiff rosettes of dark green, spiny foliage and reproducing freely from runners in the same way as strawberry plants.

Eichhornia crassipes (water hyacinth) increases in the same manner. However, with this gorgeous, free-floating aquatic the young plants are of much greater importance, as they not only increase the species numerically, but ensure its safe passage through the winter. Eichhornia crumbles at the first touch of frost and must, therefore, be given protection. Unfortunately, old plants do not over-winter successfully. Planting young stock in a pan or tray of very wet mud and keeping it frost-free in a light window or greenhouse is the only recommended course of action. Although a plant or two floated in a tropical aquarium would doubtless survive as well.

All this fuss for a plant which can only be enjoyed in the pool from June until September may seem rather tiresome. But it is really worthwhile, for the blossoms are like lovely exotic blue and lilac orchids. They are borne on short, stiff spikes and arise from amongst clusters of

Stratiotes aloides

dark green leaves with grossly inflated bases. These look like small green balloons and being full of tiny air pockets enable the plant to float successfully.

The various utricularias are not quite so sophisticated, although they do hold the dubious distinction of being one of the few carnivorous aquatic plants. At first glance one would think them to be akin to submerged oxygenating plants like myriophyllum and ceratophyllum, having very similar much-divided filigree foliage. However, lurking amongst this seemingly inoffensive green tangle are small bladders which ensnare and ingest all manner of aquatic insect life.

Utricularias do not float on the surface of the water, but just beneath it, only their flower spikes venturing above. In most species these appear during late summer and look superficially like those of an antirrhinum, but more sparsely distributed along the flower spikes.

In our native *Utricularia vulgaris* (greater bladderwort) they are rich golden yellow, while in other less common species, like *U.neglecta* and *U.inflata*, they may vary between bright yellow and pale primrose.

Finally, no mention of floating plants would be complete without *Trapa natans* (water chestnut). Although strictly speaking an annual, this handsome plant with its neat rosettes of dark green, rhomboidal, floating leaves and striking creamy-white blossoms, is usually self-perpetuating. As summer fades it produces liberal quantities of hardy, black, spiny nuts which fall to the bottom of the pool for the winter, yielding fresh young plants the next spring. It is useful to collect some of these over-wintering nuts and store them in a jar of water so that plants can be started off earlier in the season. But be sure not to allow the nuts to dry out as they rapidly lose their viability.

Marginal Plants

Harbingers of spring

Although most aquatic plants lie low until the lengthening days of early summer, there are a few hardy characters that will withstand the chill breezes of spring to brighten up the poolside and give a taste of what is to come.

Marsh marigolds are the first to show their faces, especially *Caltha palustris* (kingcup) smothered in single blossoms of glistening gold. An adaptable plant, this will grow in anything from moist soil to 20cm of water, but always makes a more compact plant in shallow conditions. A not uncommon native, this starts flowering as early as March and will usually continue until May. Even when not in flower it is quite attractive, forming neat rounded hummocks of dark green foliage.

Its double form *C.palustris* 'Flore Pleno' is even more compact, with bright golden, waxy flowers like miniature pompon chrysanthemums which completely obscure its bold, dark green foliage. The single white form *C.palustris alba* is not so inspiring and much over-rated by both nurserymen and the media. It is true that when well grown it looks very nice. However, to grow it properly requires constant vigilance, for it is prone to mildew and in a very short time becomes stunted and distorted. Why this should be is difficult to say, for if other caltha species and varieties are grown close by they are seldom affected.

Those who require a really good white marsh marigold need look no further than *C.leptosepala* (mountain marigold). This has expansive blooms with just a hint of silver and splendid rich green foliage. It is somewhat larger than *C.palustris alba*, and its variety *grandiflora* is really quite huge.

The giant of the family though is *C.polypetala* (Himalayan marsh marigold). Frequently attaining a height of 90cm with immense leaves 25cm across and great bunches of golden blossoms, this is a magnificent subject for the larger pool. It can be grown successfully in

Caltha palustris

the smaller water garden, but its considerable stature and brightly coloured flowers tend to be rather overwhelming.

As they start flowering at least a month before anything else, we tend to regard calthas as spot or specimen plants, but I get a splendid effect by associating the shorter growing kinds with *Myosotis scorpioides* (water forget-me-not). This moisture-loving relative of that much-loved inhabitant of old cottage gardens does not flower until the calthas are almost over, but its slender, scrambling foliage gains from the body given to it by the bold, scalloped leaves of its neighbour and, in turn, disguises the latter's untidy basal growth. An added bonus comes in a late spring when the marsh marigold is a little retarded, for then both erupt at the same time. The bright waxy blossoms of the calthas rising out of dark leaves with the starry, ultramarine flowers of myosotis sparkling between. Even in a normal season the final fling of the caltha will coincide with the first flush of forget-me-not blossom. These are not to be despised when grown alone, for they are freely produced and create an attractive blue haze for much of the summer.

Menyanthes trifoliata (bog bean) can be associated with myosotis in a similar manner, but with less startling results. Its amenable mode of growth permits it to associate happily amongst clump-forming plants, its stark broad bean-like leaves creating a pleasing contrast. Although looking like a bean it is not a legume, a fact confirmed during April and May when it thrusts up dense clusters of quaint white or pinkish fringed blossoms.

Calla palustris (bog arum) grows in precisely the same manner as menyanthes, spreading by means of thick green creeping rhizomes. Fortunately, these are clothed more

Myosotis scorpiodes (palustris syn.), the water forget-me-not.

Menyanthes trifoliata, the bog bean.

liberally with foliage and it is thus an excellent plant for disguising the harsh edge of the pool. Its dark green, heart-shaped leaves are bold and glossy, and during late spring and early summer become littered with tiny white papery spathes not unlike those of the florist's arum. However, this is not its main attraction, for these are followed during autumn by stout spikes of striking red berries.

Lysichitums (skunk cabbages) belong to the arum family as well, but are grown for their immense spathes which are produced during April well in advance of their foliage. In the North American *Lysichitum americanum* they are bright yellow and of a thick

Lysichitum americanum

Iris versicolor

parchment-like texture, while those of the Asiatic *L.camtschatcense* are pure white and almost translucent. Both produce large clumps of bright green, cabbagy leaves which are of considerable architectural merit.

Poolside plants of summer

The garden pool in summer belongs to the waterlilies and I am always rather worried about planting brightly coloured marginal subjects which flower at the same time and vie with them for attention. It is not that waterlilies have an exclusive right to bloom alone, but they always look better in solitary splendour surrounded by clear water with a backdrop of rushes. So bear this in mind when planning your planting and let the more startling marginal plants mingle with reeds and rushes so that they do not shout for attention.

Irises are the only group of summer flowering aquatics which can safely be planted in sizable groups, for they flower during June and are well past their best when the parade of waterlilies begins. Indeed, they always seem to me to be standing to attention ready to herald the waterlilies' arrival.

There are innumerable irises suited to damp and aquatic conditions and much confusion exists as to which will grow where. This has arisen through the popularity of two Asiatic species of similar appearance and which have doubtless hybridised as well.

The true aquatic species is the beautiful blue *Iris laevigata*, a fine marginal plant which will grow successfully in up to 15cm of water. The purple-flowered *I.kaempferi* will do so too, but only for the summer as it requires just moist conditions in the autumn and winter. Being submerged at that time of the year is certain to bring about disaster, so treat it as a moisture-loving

Veronica beccabunga, a useful scrambling plant for masking the edge of a pool.

Mentha aquatica, the water mint.

perennial. Distinguishing the two when not in flower is quite easy, for the leaves of *I.laevigata* are always smooth whereas those of *I.kaempferi* have a prominent midrib.

I find *I.laevigata* the most acceptable aquatic iris, for it is both charming and unpretentious, unlike many of its cultivars. But these are liked by some and are certainly fine examples of the plant breeders' art. 'Monstrosa' is the most spectacular with expansive blossoms of violet and white, while 'Rose Queen' has slender flowers of soft rose pink. 'Alba' is cool icy white and the variety known variously as 'Elegantissima' and 'Variegata' has foliage vertically striped with cream.

The American version of *I.laevigata* is called *I.versicolor*. Although not to everyone's taste, I like its finely sculptured blossoms of violet and purple with their conspicuous yellow patches. Its variety 'Kermesina' is even more lovely, with superb blooms of a gorgeous shade of deep plum.

Our native water iris is the tall and ungainly *I.pseudacorus* (yellow flag). An amiable plant it is true, but rather too coarse and vigorous for the average garden pool. Its more refined cultivar 'Golden Queen' should be accommodated where space allows and the soft primrose form *bastardi* ought to receive consideration, but where space is at a premium I would go for the golden and green variegated foliage variety 'Variegata'.

Hypericum elodes is a useful plant to mix with irises, for it is a scrambler and will smother the bare areas between their upright fans of leaves with a dense carpet of more or less evergreen foliage. From July until September this is illuminated with myriad tiny, twinkling, golden blossoms like much refined miniatures of its landlubber cousin *H.calycinum* (rose of sharon).

Veronica beccabunga (brooklime) fulfils a similar role, sprawling in all directions with procumbent stems and dark green leaves. These persist almost all year round and make the plant especially valuable for masking the pool edge. Indeed, a combination of veronica and *Hypericum elodes* is probably the most satisfactory for this purpose.

Veronica beccabunga flowers for most of the summer, and although its slender spikes of dark blue flowers with conspicuous white eyes are not spectacular, they are produced in sufficient quantities to be noticed. The only problem to be encountered with veronica is its over-exuberance which necessitates it being cut back hard each spring. Rather than retain the old plants I prefer to push vigorous young shoots into the mud once growth commences and then remove the older clumps and discard them.

The same procedure is useful for *Mentha aquatica* (water mint) for this, too, is exceedingly vigorous and will oust less resilient neighbours when given the opportunity. Like veronica it grows freely from cuttings and makes far better growth from these than aged rootstocks. In common with other mints it has strongly aromatic foliage which tends to be rather hairy and is almost completely obscured in late summer by dense whorls of lilac-pink flowers like miniature powder-puffs.

Although I have a strong affection for mentha, I am always reluctant to plant it in a small pond as it is only too ready to dominate. For aromatic foliage I would rather have *Preslia cervina*, a little known yet easily grown plant which is much better mannered. It spreads politely with slender stems clothed in small, dark green, lanceolate leaves which during late spring give rise to stiff whorled spikes of blue or lilac blossoms. I deeply regret it not being

Houttuynia cordata 'Plena', a valuable poolside carpeting plant.

Sagittaria sagittiflora 'Flore Pleno', the arrowhead.

more widely grown, for it is a lovely little thing and so easily propagated from cuttings. So if you come upon a plant be generous and spread it about a bit, for it is a most welcome addition to the water garden.

So is *Mimulus ringens*, a truly aquatic musk with delicate blue flowers. Unlike the mimulus which we grow in the bog garden or damp border, this has slender, much branched stems 45cm high and unexpectedly narrow leaves. It will grow from seed in the same manner as the popular *M.cupreus* and *luteus* and their colourful strains, but is more easily increased by short cuttings just pushed in the mud. Again this has much to commend it, for fresh young stock seems to be much freer flowering and makes tidier clumps of foliage.

Mimulus ringens always looks a bit helpless on its own so I like to back it up with something more substantial. *Houttuynia cordata* is a favourite as this is a neat carpeting plant with handsome bluish-green, heart-shaped foliage and complimentary blossoms of creamy white. The double form 'Plena' is the best of all because the flowers are more substantial and its rate of growth more restrained.

Saururus cernuus (lizard's tail) can be used in the same manner if you can bear its irregular clumps of rounded leaves and strange sprays of whitish blossoms. I spend all summer wondering why ever I planted it and just as I think I will throw it away it takes on rich autumnal tints and wins a reprieve. These tints vary from one year to another, but their intensity seems to be increased by the severity of the weather.

Sagittarias are plants which no gardener can have any qualms about, for they are worth growing for their superb arrow-shaped foliage alone. This varies in shape and size according to the variety grown, but

Mimulus ringens

Sagittaria japonica produces the finest and broadest arrows of all. Not content with this it also thrusts up spikes of snow-white flowers with bright yellow centres which, in its double form 'Flore Pleno' are completely obscured by the fullness of the petals.

Sagittaria sagittifolia is closely allied to *S.japonica* and some botanists contend that one is just another form of the other. However, this is of little account, for although similar they are really quite different, the leaves of *S.sagittifolia* being more acutely arrow shaped and its white blossoms having centres of black and crimson.

No such confusion is caused by *S.latifolia*, for unlike those previously described, which scarcely exceed 60cm in height, this monster soars to

Saururus cernuus, lizard's tail.

well over a metre. It is too large for most pools, but when in a suitable setting is quite imposing. The ordinary species is the easiest to come by and has attractive sprays of single white flowers, while the cultivar 'Flore Pleno' is fully double.

All sagittarias grow and increase from turions or bulbils, which in the case of the varieties just mentioned are about the size of a pigeon's egg.

Unfortunately, these are attractive to ducks which, if given the opportunity, will scoop them out of the mud and devour them with great relish. Thus their popular name 'duck potato'. In some localities it may be necessary to protect the area where they are growing with a piece of fine mesh wire netting. Once the emerging foliage is about 10cm high and the plants well rooted they

should not be unduly troubled.

Another aquatic with arrow shaped foliage is peltandra. This is a close relative of the arum and produces small spathes of similar appearance. In the commonest species *Peltandra alba*, these are white, or sometimes flushed with green, whereas those of the more diminutive *P.virginica* are narrower and a bright pea green. Not a

An unexpected oasis set against a backdrop of decorative shrubs and lawn.

Marginal Plants

spectacular plant for the poolside, but a most interesting acquisition whose spathes will be valued by the flower arranger.

I am not usually enthusiastic about buttercups, but I would not be without the closely related *Ranunculus lingua* (greater spearwort), for this cheerful fellow gives untold pleasure from early spring until late summer. Few plants in the winter water garden can persuade the gardener that spring is just around the corner better than this. For there in the winter beneath the ice are gorgeous green and rose leaves just bursting with life. When the ice melts in March they are well away, the clusters of leaves expanding into green and rose spears which thrust through the water and erupt in the spring sunshine into a cascade of purplish-green foliage. This ages to dark green and is then showered with glistening golden blossoms the size of a twopenny piece. A really fine plant which in the popularly grown octaploid variant 'Grandiflora' is supreme.

Some say it is too invasive for the garden pool, but I would disagree. If unwanted shoots are removed in the spring it is not difficult to keep within bounds. Now if one were to complain about the alismas (water plantains) there might be some justification as these do scatter their seed rather freely. Nevertheless, they are worthy additions to the pool and providing one is aware of the problem and removes the flower spikes immediately they fade there is no cause for alarm. Indeed, if carefully dried these flower spikes will become quite woody and their symmetrical spire-like form can be utilised to advantage in floral decorations.

There are four species of alisma commonly cultivated, but only two are of sufficient merit to justify their place in the modern garden pool.

Pontederia cordata provides poolside colour until the first frosts.

Our native *Alisma plantago-aquatica* is the most familiar with its handsome ovate leaves and towering panicles of pink or white flowers a metre or more high. The North American *A.parviflora* is a trifle more refined and sports fine rounded foliage and shorter spires of pink or white blossoms. Both species flower for much of the summer, their billowing sprays of flowers being a suitable foil for more stately characters like *Pontederia cordata* (pickerel).

An immensely valuable plant on account of its late summer and early autumn flowering, pontederia can be thoroughly recommended for any shape or size of pool. Its superb glossy ovate or lanceolate foliage of a rich green hue earns it a place at the poolside, but the bold spikes of soft blue flowers which appear from amongst leafy bracts are its crowning glory. But be sure you get the shorter growing *P.cordata*, for some nurserymen offer a very similar species called *P.lanceolata* which, in conditions to its liking, may attain a height of upwards of a metre.

Sedges, reeds and rushes

To the newcomer to water gardening one rush may seem very much like another, and sedges and reeds pose considerable problems as it is difficult to decide where one starts and the other ends. Broadly speaking, sedges are the grassy marginal plants with small, congested, grass-like seed heads, while rushes generally have cylindrical foliage and reeds broad, fleshy leaves. This is technically how they are separated, but our forebears were obviously not aware of these subtle differences and popular names which are, strictly speaking, incorrect have attained wide popularity. In practical terms we may consider that all plants described under this heading have vertical grassy foliage which is their main attribute, their flower spikes being of secondary or little importance.

Mention water plants and bulrushes always spring to mind, those stately plants with broad, glaucous-green foliage and chocolate-brown, poker-like fruiting heads. But these are not really bulrushes, for the true bulrush is *Scirpus lacustris*. These are reed maces.

There are a number of reed maces to choose from, but unless there is plenty of room to spare the native *Typha angustifolia* and *T.latifolia* should be avoided. I would never grow them in a pool lined with polythene either, for they spread by creeping rhizomes which have sharp, spear-like growing points capable of puncturing a liner. Indeed, the cultivation of these two lovable rogues is beset with problems as they are both too vigorous and too tall for most situations. When grown in the comparative safety of a basket they continually topple over, and if given full rein on the marginal shelf will interfere with their neighbours.

For a really good, well-behaved reed mace we must turn to *T.laxmannii* which in most nursery catalogues still languishes under the outmoded name of *T.stenophylla*. This grows little more than a metre high and has slender, willowy leaves and attractive, rich brown pokers. But in the smaller pool this is still too large and is better replaced by *T.minima*. Rarely exceeding 45cm in height, this complete miniature could have come straight out of Lilliput. It has somewhat grassy foliage of a bluish-green hue and short, chunky flower spikes.

The true bulrush, as represented by *Scirpus lacustris*, is a rather demure character with slender, dark

Typha minima, the miniature reed mace.

Scirpus 'Zebrinus', zebra rush.

green, cylindrical, needle-like stems a metre or more high and tiny, pendant tassels of reddish-brown flowers. It is useful as a foil for more cheerful aquatics and can be used to good effect in creating height in a formal scheme. But I would always go for the steely-blue *S.tabernaemontani* as it has more substantial foliage with an attractive mealy bloom.

Not only is *S.tabernaemontani* a better looking plant, but a progenitor of two of the finest foliage aquatics. The cultivar 'Zebrinus' (zebra rush) is the most striking as it has foliage alternatively barred with green and white. As with most variegated plants green stems are occasionally produced and these must be removed immediately they are noticed to prevent them outgrowing the variegated part.

The variety 'Albescens' is also attributed to *S.tabernaemontani*, although there is considerable speculation as to its origin. Certainly it has the same pleasant habit, but with lovely sulphureous-white stems conspicuously marked with thin longitudinal stripes of green. It does not appear to be as hardy as its colleagues, so the old stems should be bent over the crown for the winter and a generous layer of bracken or straw secured over it as well. In fact, if it is growing in a basket and can be easily removed intact from the pool, it can be stood in a cool, frost-free shed and just kept moist until the following spring without coming to any harm.

The various species of juncus are of similar habit to scirpus, but generally much shorter growing and owing to their prolific seeding and creeping capabilities, excluded from the garden pool. Two mutants of the native *Juncus effusus* (soft rush), however, are worthy of attention and in common with the majority of choice garden plants, rather slow to reproduce.

The most interesting mutant is *J.effusus* 'Spiralis' a curiously malformed plant with slender cylindrical stems which grow in a corkscrew fashion such as is seen in the corkscrew willow, *Salix matsudana* 'Tortuosa'. The other is a golden and green barred version of the species known variously as 'Vittatus' and 'Aureo-striatus'. Unfortunately, this is a very weak grower which is easily overtaken by its plain green foliage and is in constant need of attention.

When variegated foliage is required in a plant that has vigour and seldom throws unwanted green shoots, then *Glyceria maxima variegata* provides the answer. Strictly speaking, this does not belong here as it is really a grass, but its overall aspect is the same as a rush or sedge and it certainly serves the same purpose. It is a handsome plant, tolerant of damp conditions or up to 15cm of water and has cream and green striped foliage which is infused with a deep rose flush during early spring.

The variegated form of *Acorus calamus* has the same deep pinkish infusion in its emerging shoots, but foliage which ultimately attains the character and proportions of an iris. Again, this is not strictly speaking a rush or reed, although most gardeners would allow those terms to embrace it. It is, in fact, a rather bizarre member of the arum family with tiny, greenish, horn-like inflorescences which appear amongst the leaves. These are of little significance and can be barely discerned amongst the shiny fresh green foliage of ordinary *A.calamus*. Despite the flowers being of little consequence, both *A.calamus* and *A.c.* 'Variegatus' are well worth growing, not just for the handsome appearance of their foliage, but its rich tangerine fragrance.

This is not apparent in the smaller kinds which are grown variously under the names of *A.gramineus* and *A.pusillus*. These are dwarf species with slender, dark green, sword-like leaves no more than 25cm high which, in the variegated kinds, are boldly striped with yellow. They are neat clump-forming plants and ideally suited to the rock pool or sink garden.

A lot of confusion exists amongst these as to which are distinct species and which are mere variants, but this has not spread itself into the nursery trade and the pool owner who buys a plant under either *A.gramineus* or *A.pusillus* is almost certainly purchasing a dwarf kind of exceptional merit.

No one is likely to get into a muddle over the status of *Butomus*

Glyceria maxima variegata

Acorus calamus has a rich tangerine fragrance.

umbellatus (flowering rush), as this striking plant is the sole member of the family with no forms, variants or allied species. It is a quite unique plant with narrow, triquetrous foliage interspersed during late summer with spreading umbels of dainty rose-pink blossoms. These are often in evidence at the same time as the soft blue flower spikes of *Pontederia cordata* and a mixed planting of these two is something to behold. Not only are the pastel shades of their flowers complementary, but their contrasting leaf growths make a remarkable combination.

Eriophorum angustifolium (cotton grass) is another plant which can create an effect. Not necessarily in association with any other species, for with its stiff grassy foliage sprinkled in early summer with silky, cotton wool-like, seeding heads, it is a picture in itself. Upwards of twenty different species of eriophorum have been described, but only *E.angustifolium* and the more mundane *E.latifolium* are cultivated. Both require acidic soil and water if they are to flourish and seem to prefer a position out of full sun.

The sedges prosper under almost any conditions, particularly the native kinds like *Carex pendula*. This tall and dignified plant with broad green leaves and pendulous, brownish, catkin-like flowers is particularly useful for filling an inhospitable corner in the larger water garden. For the small pool it has little use and is better replaced by one of the cultivars of *C.riparia* such as the rich golden-yellow 'Bowles' Golden' or the striking green and white 'Variegata'. To be truthful few of the carex species have much to offer the modern water garden, and although a number are offered by aquatics specialists, none other than those described should be afforded a position. There are many

Butomus umbellatus

more far superior leafy marginals.

A prime example is *Cyperus longus* (sweet galingale). A larger and coarser version of the popular florist's umbrella plant (*Cyperus alternifolius*), this is invaluable for interspersing as a pleasant foil amongst more colourful subjects. Where moist ground reaches down to the pool it can really be exploited, for *C.longus* is never happier than when marching into the pool from damp ground. In a natural pool where erosion is a problem then cyperus is the perfect stabiliser.

It is not bad looking either, with terminal umbels of stiff, spiky leaves which radiate from the stem like the ribs of an umbrella. Under suitable conditions it will grow more than a metre high, and if that is too tall for your particular purpose, then try the smaller growing *C.vegetus*. This has

Eriophorum angustifolium, cotton grass.

broader foliage than *C.longus*, borne in typical fashion, and during late summer is surmounted by tufted spikelets of reddish-mahogany flowers.

Finally, no review of sedges, reeds or rushes would be complete without mentioning *Sparganium ramosum* (bur reed). Not because it is something special, although it does have a peculiar charm of its own, but because it is not infrequently sold to the unsuspecting pool owner. Unfortunately, sparganium looks really strong and attractive in its formative life and this is very tempting to the nurseryman. It also develops quite pleasing foliage and produces strange, bur-like, seed heads. However, it is neither of these that present problems, but the invasive rootstock which sends shoots up in all directions. This spreads out an armoury of rhizomes, each with a very sharp growing point which will quickly puncture a pool liner.

Cyperus longus, sweet galingale.

1. *Veronica beccabunga*
2. *Caltha palustris* 'Flore Pleno'
3. *Pontederia cordata*
4. *Butomus umbellatus*
5. *Iris laevigata*
6. *Caltha leptosepala*
7. *Sagittaria japonica*
8. *Menyanthes trifoliata*
9. *Iris laevigata* 'Rose Queen'
10. *Calla palustris*
11. *Scirpus tabernaemontani* 'Zebrinus'
12. *Mentha aquatica*
13. *Aponogeton distachyus*
14. *Lagarosiphon major* (*Elodea crispa*)
15. *Nymphaea* 'Rose Arey'
16. *Myriophyllum spicatum*

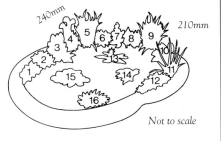

Not to scale

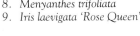

The design of this informal pool incorporates a variety of leaf forms, habits and flowering times, yet still allows for a certain amount of reflection in the water.

Each plant represents one basket, the quantity of plants included being immaterial, except in the case of the lagarosiphon and myriophyllum which should be planted twelve bunches to a basket to give a correct balance.

Plants for the Bog Garden

Spring flowering bog plants

While the pool is dull and lifeless during the winter and early spring, the bog garden can retain our interest. Indeed, there are so many different species of moisture-loving perennials that the gardener with a reasonable amount of space has no excuse for not having something in flower at every season of the year.

Take *Petasites fragrans* (winter heliotrope) for instance. This comes into flower as early, or late, as November and carries on right into March. Its fragrant, lilac-pink blossoms are borne in dense clusters and succeeded by long-stalked, roundish leaves. The larger

Cardamine pratensis

P. japonicus is quite widely grown, but as it has immense, cabbagy foliage well over a metre high it cannot be seriously considered for the smaller garden. However, where space can be spared it is well worth having, its large, crowded heads of scentless white blossoms appearing well in advance of the foliage.

The early spring flowering *Peltiphyllum peltatum* is of similar aspect but considerably smaller, its globular heads of soft pink blooms being carried on slender stems 45cm high. These appear before the handsome, rounded, bronze-green leaves which are proudly supported on centrally placed leaf stalks.

The charming *Cardamine pratensis* (cuckoo flower) flowers at around the same time, although it does not associate well with peltiphyllum. Growing to a height of 30cm, this delightful native has attractive pinnate foliage and delicate lilac blossoms, which, in the more compact *flore-plena*, are fully double. Like a number of other bog garden subjects, cardamine will grow well in either sun or shade.

This could also be said about the moisture-loving primulas, although one or two prefer a little dappled shade. The first species to flower are the tiny *Primula rosea* and military-looking *P. denticulata*. Both provide a

Petasites japonicus

bold splash of colour at the poolside during March and April and are easily grown in constantly moist conditions.

Primula rosea never gets more than 15cm high and carries a profusion of intense rose-pink blossoms above tufts of freshly emerging bronze-green foliage which ages to soft green. The cultivar 'Delight' is even more lovely and should be grown whenever possible.

Several selections of *P. denticulata* have been made, but none can compare with the natural blue and lilac shades of the species. The white

Interesting plant associations frame the mirror-like surface of the water.

form *alba*, lilac-purple and mealy-leafed *cashmireana*, and the various red and mauve strains always looked rather artificial to me. In fact, the structure of the flower heads, which appear as tight rounded clusters on short stout stems, are not at all easy to incorporate into the general garden scene. Certainly *P.denticulata* would present considerable difficulties if it flowered later in the year and had to vie with other plants for attention. As it is now, it can be allowed to flower alone in solitary splendour.

The same sort of problem arises with the later flowering *P.vialii*, a striking plant with neat spikes of red and lilac blooms, both in shape and contrast like those of a red hot poker. Even though other plants crave for attention, this extraordinary primula should be given pride of place, being planted with a background of subtle greens such as can be provided by hardy ferns. It is a truly remarkable plant with a rather temperamental nature, but well worth trying to tame.

Candelabra primulas are good-natured and easily placed. Their handsome tiered whorls of blossoms being easy on the eye and readily conforming to most surroundings. They are not solitary plants though, and must be planted boldly in clumps or drifts. Most kinds start flowering during early May and continue well into the summer.

I like *P.aurantiaca* with its bright reddish-orange flowers. The purplish-red *P.japonica* and its cultivars 'Postford White' and 'Miller's Crimson', together with the lovely magenta *P.pulverulenta* with its attractive mealy stems. 'Bartley Strain' is derived from *P.pulverulenta* and yields a range of pastel shades which extend from buff through peach to pink, while the later flowering *P.bulleyana* has uniform flowers of orange in dense tiered

Primula beesiana

Primula viallii

whorls. *Primula beesiana* and *P.burmanica* have blossoms in rosy-purple shades and complete the range of easily grown candelabra varieties.

Primula florindae (Himalayan cowslip) looks rather like an overgrown cowslip and has pendant, sulphureous bells on stems a metre or so high. These arise from amongst coarse, cabbagy leaves which have a delicious aroma. *Primula sikkimensis* is almost identical, but with much smaller, sweetly scented, soft yellow blossoms, while the more refined *P.microdonta alpicola* and its deep mauve variety *violacea* grow in a similar fashion. These two have much smoother foliage and are readily distinguished by their liberal coating of white or yellowish farina which covers the leaves and extends up the flower stems. Neither grows more than 45cm high and each gives a touch of class to the bog garden.

This can also be provided by the recently popularised *P.sieboldii* and its varieties. Although the enthusiasm with which nurserymen are propagating and distributing them tends to lead me to think that in a year or two they will be as common as formations of china ducks up the living-room wall were in the 1950's. I would not wish to halt their progress by such terse comments, but I feel that there is a danger in a plant achieving instant success, for then all manner of inferior forms are distributed.

Good named varieties in pink and white shades, preferably purchased growing in pots and in flower are the safest means of ensuring a good show. They produce open floppy blossoms on stems scarcely 30cm high which peep out from amongst lovely soft crimpled foliage.

Primula waltonii grows just a little taller and has clustered flowers of deep port wine red, while *P.cock-*

Primula pulverulenta

burniana is short and compact with blossoms of intense orange-scarlet. These two and *P.sieboldii* always grow more satisfactorily in light shade and, although requiring moist conditions, will not tolerate the really wet situations enjoyed by *P.florindae* and *P.sikkimensis*.

Trollius are grand for associating with primulas. Coming into flower variously from late April until mid June, they make a brave show with their incurved heads of bright yellow or orange blossoms on strong wiry stems. Their dark green lobed foliage belies their close affinity with the buttercups, but, fortunately, they do not have the same invasive tendencies. In fact, they are all quite restrained and form tidy hummocks of foliage.

Trollius and Primula make a grand association

The soft yellow *Trollius europaeus* and the greatly under-rated rich golden *T.asiaticus* are the parents of most modern hybrids, with the occasional intervention of *T.sinensis*. Although all three are of garden merit, their progeny are much improved and consequently more widely planted. 'Fire Globe' is deep orange, 'Orange Princess' a trifle paler, while 'Canary Bird' is rich yellow.

Summer flowering bog plants

Having just described a selection of the earlier flowering bog garden plants, I perhaps ought to mention that a number of these will provide colour well into the summer too. Plants do not recognise the line I have drawn separating spring flowering kinds from summer blooming varieties and thus some will encroach upon the season of the other, particularly in years where weather conditions are unusual. So, broadly speaking, it can be taken that those I have selected for the spring garden will be over by the time the true aquatics start making a show. Therefore, their placement in the bog garden is not quite so critical as those I will now describe. For these flower in unison with marginal plants and waterlilies and need careful positioning if they are not to spoil the overall picture.

Just as aquatic irises can be used to great effect around the margins of the pool, their moisture-loving counterparts can be exploited in the bog garden. I have already mentioned the lovely purple-flowered *Iris kaempferi* when discussing its confusion with the truly aquatic *I.laevigata*. However, I only wrote a couple of words about this, when a couple of pages would be insufficient to extol the virtues of this beautiful plant and its myriad varieties.

For ordinary garden decoration a good mixed strain is difficult to beat. Cultivars with fancy Japanese names have been imported in considerable numbers in recent years and these are of uniform colour and habit. However, beware of the 'Higo' strain. An amazing selection of brightly-coloured sorts with huge clematis-like flowers which look like exotic tropical butterflies at rest on slender sword-like foliage.

These are really magnificent irises, but totally unsuited to general garden use. Their flower heads are so large that the wind snaps them off and heavy rain does little to aid their beauty. 'Higo' irises were developed by the Japanese for the florist and for exhibiting. They were not intended to withstand the rough and tumble of the garden, being grown almost exclusively in pots and afforded considerable protection from the elements.

Iris sibirica and its cultivars thrive in most situations, not resenting an alkaline soil in the same way as do *I.kaempferi,* and being more tolerant of the moisture level of their growing medium. Indeed, *I.sibirica* can be grown reasonably successfully under ordinary border conditions and will survive equally well when temporarily immersed in water.

Typical *I.sibirica* has narrow grassy foliage and finely sculptured blue flowers which appear during June and the early part of July. These are not over-bearing like some of the modern *I.kaempferi* hybrids and conform readily to any planting scheme. Its cultivars are rather more boisterous, but retain their dignity and form neat clumps no more than 60-70cm high. I like 'Blue Moon', 'Snow Queen' and the purple-flowered 'Caesar'. 'Mrs Saunders' has dark blue flowers with white reticulations, while 'Emperor' is of the deepest violet-blue. 'Perry's Pigmy' is deep blue or violet and being less than half the size of the

Iris sibirica

Lysimachia nummularia, creeping jenny.

others is an invaluable plant for the smaller water garden.

The delightful little Chinese *I.bulleyana* can also be recommended when space is at a premium. Scarcely more than 40cm high, it produces tufts of grassy foliage sprinkled with delicate, rich blue blossoms. These put one in mind of *I.setosa*, except that this adaptable species is slightly dwarfer with bold, broad, sword-like leaves. Innumerable forms of *I.setosa* have crept into cultivation from time to time. Of these the compact variety *nana* is an absolute gem. Growing no more than 15cm high this has stout fans of leaves and full size flowers of the same incomparable blue.

Iris ochroleuca is one of the more vigorous bog garden species with handsome glaucous foliage and contrasting flowers of white and gold. It grows more than a metre high, and although not really a plant for the smaller garden, where it can be accommodated it provides excellent background material. The equally robust *I.aurea* is sometimes put to the same use. While its deep yellow blooms are just as striking, its foliage is more sombre and lacks the stiff architectural form displayed by that of *I.ochroleuca*.

As noted earlier when discussing aquatic irises, they always benefit visually from an association with a scrambling or creeping subject. And what better to use than *Lysimachia nummularia* (creeping jenny). A plant of many parts, this more or less evergreen carpeter smothers the soil with pleasant rounded leaves, which in the cultivar 'Aurea' are rich glowing yellow. Throughout June and July the sprawling tangle of stems are host to innumerable bright yellow flowers the shape and size of a common buttercup.

Being a not uncommon native, some people regard *L.nummularia* with suspicion. This is unfortunate, for it is one of the most adaptable plants for bog garden and poolside planting. Not only does it provide ground cover between taller growing plants, but can be used successfully to mask the edge of the pool where it meets the surrounding ground. It has no qualms about entering the water either, for here it will produce roots quite freely from its leaf joints. If some of this semi-aquatic growth is removed and planted in the bottom of the pool it will grow and serve as a submerged oxygenating plant, although it will not flower. But do not try to submerge ordinary growth as this will almost certainly perish. It seems to need a period of adaptation before becoming a stable submerged plant.

A number of other lysimachia species are recommended for the bog garden from time to time. However, these are coarse clump-forming plants 60cm or more high and better suited to stream or riverside planting. If one desires the upright spire-like growth so characteristic of those species, then it is better to select a cultivar or two from the range offered by *Lythrum salicaria* (purple loosestrife).

This is not to say that *L.salicaria* itself is of little value, for its stiff bushy clumps of foliage support deep rose-purple blossoms which put on quite a show from July until September. It is just that I think the cultivars are better for the modern garden. They are more compact, generally shorter, and embrace a colour range that passes from purple through rose-red to pink. I would choose the lovely soft pink 'Robert', or delicate rose 'Lady Sackville' and it would be difficult to deny a place to 'The Beacon' with its well-proportioned spikes of rich rosy-red.

Astilbes are equally valuable, particularly some of the compact modern cultivars. These fit in with any design as they grow little more than 75cm high and are only available in friendly pastel shades. Their feathery plumes of flowers and attractive divided leaves associate with most other plants, which means that they can be planted freely without becoming obtrusive and offending the eye.

'White Gloria' with its contrasting dark green foliage is my favourite, although the aptly named 'Peach Blossom' runs it a close second. The bright crimson 'Fanal', 'Red Sentinel', and lilac-pink 'Cattleya' also rate highly with me. As do the tiny pink-flowered cultivars of *Astilbe crispa* – 'Perkeo' and 'Lilliput'. These have congested tufts of dark green crinkled foliage and only grow 15cm high. But the real king of the miniatures is *A.chinensis* 'Pumila'. Slightly taller than the *A.crispa* cultivars, this produces prostrate tufts of dark green leaves and beautifully proportioned spires of purplish-rose flowers.

Aruncus sylvester is a majestic relative of the astilbe, forming immense clumps of luxuriant foliage and towering plumes of creamy-white flowers a couple of metres high. It is often grown in the bog garden where its huge mounds of foliage dwarf and smother less vigorous neighbours. In such a situation it is totally out of keeping. I like to see it planted in solitary splendour at the edge of the pool where it can be reflected in the cool glassy stillness of the water. If surrounded on the landward side by a verdant lawn, it presents a picture of unparalleled beauty, the greens of grass and foliage complementing one another perfectly.

Before leaving astilbe and aruncus I ought to mention their forgotten relatives the filipendulas. The well-loved *Filipendula ulmaria* (meadow sweet) is a frequent inhabitant of stream sides and ditches throughout Great Britain. Even if sweetly scented and quite charming, it does not really deserve a place in the bog garden. Especially when the double form *flore-plena* and golden-leafed 'Aurea' can be grown. There are many other species worthy of consideration if you have a large garden, for most of them grow to more than a metre high and half as much through. Only the dainty *F.hexapetala* (dropwort) in its double form is worth considering, for this has delicate fern-like foliage and crowded heads of cool icy-white blossoms. These are only in evidence during June and July, but the splendid filigree foliage persists for much of the year and is a constant delight.

The leaves of the perennial lobelias can also make a significant contribution. Particularly the rich beetroot-coloured one of *Lobelia fulgens*. Unlike the familiar bedding lobelias, the hardy perennial species grow in upright spiky clumps varying in height from 60cm–1m. They are not all blue flowered either, the blossoms of both *L.fulgens* and the green-leafed *L.cardinalis* being vivid red.

Lobelia vedrariensis is the tallest kind and has violet blooms and bright green leaves suffused with maroon, while the shade-loving *L.syphilitica* has rather ordinary green

Lythrum salicaria, purple loosestrife

foliage and bright blue flowers. Although flourishing well in moist conditions, they will not survive the winter in waterlogged soil. In fact with *L.cardinalis* and *L.fulgens* it is a wise precaution to over-winter a clump or two in a cold frame, for their emerging foliage is prone to damage by severe weather and particularly vulnerable to attacks from slugs and snails.

Some of the mimulus would appreciate similar protection for the winter months, especially the downy-leafed species like the bright red *Mimulus cardinalis* and lilac-pink *M.lewisii*. Even the cultivars of the bright yellow *M.luteus* and reddish-copper *M.cupreus* benefit from having a rosette or two of over-wintering foliage moved to a safe haven in case of severe winter weather.

Most mimulus grow between 25-60cm high, the modern cultivars like 'Bonfire', 'Scarlet Emperor' and 'Yellow Velvet' tending to occupy the lower end of the scale. They are all extremely showy, producing brightly coloured, antirrhinum-like flowers from the end of May until July and often again during late summer. Apart from growing well in moist conditions, a number will also spread and colonise the marginal shelves in several centimetres of water. Forms derived directly from *M.luteus* are particularly prone to doing this. Varieties like the golden 'Hose-In-Hose' in which one flower appears to be inside the other, and the incomparable large yellow-flowered 'A.T. Johnson' with its profusely spotted petals.

For the sink garden or rock pool there is a superb dwarf variety called 'Whitecroft Scarlet'. This is a remarkable plant, scarcely more than 8cm high, with mats of tiny carpeting foliage and unusual hooded blossoms of brilliant scarlet. Certainly the best dwarf plant for

the bog garden, and although not reliably perennial is easily raised from seed and will flower the first year.

Before I leave the flowering bog garden plants I must write a word or two about another unreliable perennial; *Zantedeschia aethiopica* (white arum lily). Why nurserymen and gardeners persist with this plant outdoors I will never know, for to survive the winter in this country it must be grown in at least 30cm of water. From such cold inhospitable depths it takes a long time to surface and consequently flowers very late or not at all. The only method of growing it well is to have it in a pot which is plunged in the bog garden when all danger of frost has passed. The pot and plant can then be removed to the safety of the greenhouse for the winter months. Alternatively the hardy variety 'Crowborough' can be tried, but this

is smaller and less imposing than the true florist's arum.

Ferns and foliage plants

Foliage is as important a part of the ornamental garden as flowers. Leaves in all their shapes and forms add interest, subtle variations of colour, and provide a foil for flowering subjects. In many ways foliage plants are more important than flowering ones, for they make a background or a backbone to a feature. With careful use they can also be used to frame a picture or create a focal point. The possibilities they offer are limitless and as they provide this service for much of the year they should be duly recognised.

Ferns, of course, are the cream of foliage plants. Most enjoy damp conditions and partial shade, but a few will flourish in really wet conditions in the open. They have a preference for slightly acidic soil rich

Zantedeschia aethiopica, the white arum lily, can be a challenge to grow.

in organic matter and this can be adequately catered for by incorporating liberal quantities of peat at planting time.

Osmunda regalis (royal fern) is without doubt the finest of all hardy ferns. A tall regal plant with large, leathery fronds between 1-2m high. These are lime green, but turn a rich burnished bronze in the autumn before collapsing on top of their large scaly crowns. This debris, together with a handful of straw or bracken, should be placed over each crown in order to protect the young fronds as they emerge the following spring.

It is a matter of some regret that many gardeners will be unable to find sufficient space for this marvellous plant. However, its varieties 'Undulata', with crimpled and crested fronds, and the strangely tassellated 'Cristata' (crested royal fern) are generally of more manageable proportions. Even the superb purplish-fronded 'Purpurescens' seldom grows as large as *O.regalis*.

Onoclea sensibilis (sensitive fern) can be grown in many situations as it attains a height of little more than 45cm and enjoys both damp and aquatic conditions. It can be used in much the same manner as *Cyperus longus* or *Lysimachia nummularia*, being planted in moist soil at the poolside and allowed to colonise the shallower areas. In texture and shape the fronds of onoclea have a lot in common with osmunda, but rather than growing from a scaly clump they are spread out along a black creeping rhizome. During early spring the fronds are an attractive rose-pink colour, but fade with age to pale lime green.

Matteuccia struthiopteris (ostrich feather fern) is a handsome creeper too, thrusting up bright green fronds arranged in a shuttlecock fashion around a hard scaly rootstock. Like

Matteuccia struthiopteris, the ostrich feather fern.

onoclea, this will grow in extremely wet conditions in either sun or shade. It is a good bit taller though, mature plants being almost a metre high and obviously in need of careful placing.

Most of the other ferns that enjoy wet conditions are less spectacular, but can be used for carpeting between other plants. I am thinking now of the short growing *Dryopteris cristata* (crested buckler fern), the elegant *Dryopteris palustris* (marsh buckler fern) and that classy North American woodlander *Woodwardia virginica* (Virginian chain fern).

Few other foliage plants are in the same class as ferns, except possibly the hostas. Not that they resemble ferns in any way, for they have broad, glossy, ovate or cordate leaves in innumerable shades of green, or sometimes variegated and occasionally edged with cream. Unlike ferns they produce moderately attractive bell-shaped flowers of lilac or white in graceful arching sprays.

It is a brave man who tries to separate and classify the various species and varieties of hosta. Even the botanists do not always seem able to agree. So what I will do here is describe the popular kinds under the names they are usually sold by, even though these may not strictly speaking be botanically correct.

Hosta undulata mediovariegata is probably the most commonly cultivated sort. A striking plant with slightly twisted leaves in a mixture of cream and green. Another unrelated hybrid called 'Thomas Hogg' has large, plain green leaves broadly edged with white, while the cultivar 'Aurea' sports golden foliage that fades to green with age.

But for texture and shape the plain-leafed kinds are unsurpassed.

Particularly if one looks at species like *H.sieboldiana* with its immense glaucous leaves 30cm long and almost as wide, or the elegant Japanese *H.fortunei* proudly displaying narrow, bright green leaves and graceful sprays of pale lilac blossoms. Alternatively *Hosta ventricosa* produces big, mid-green, heart-shaped leaves and surprisingly attractive mauve bell-like flowers during summer. If you only have room for one hosta you should seriously consider this one.

Foliage is unquestionably the principal attribute of the various decorative members of the rhubarb family. These are specimen plants for a focal point and useful in creating bold architectural effects. *Rheum palmatum* is unquestionably the best and will tolerate really wet conditions. It is also the most impressive species with expansive fresh green foliage and spikes of creamy blossoms of 2m high. Its cut-leafed form *tanguticum* has a purplish infusion and attractive deeply cut foliage, while 'Bowles' Crimson' is of typical form, but with spires of crimson flowers and leaves with a strong purplish-red cast.

It would be difficult to write about foliage plants for the bog garden without giving *Gunnera manicata* a mention, even though it is much too large for most gardens. Being the largest herbaceous subject capable of cultivation outdoors in Great Britain, and with its immense rhubarb-like foliage it can create quite dramatic effects. When growing contentedly it will produce leaves up to 1.5m across on stout prickly leaf stalks some 2m high. Its strange inflorescence is like a large reddish-green bottle brush and appears beneath the foliage during late summer.

A native of Brazil, gunnera is reliably hardy in most localities, but during autumn benefits from having its withered leaves inverted over the huge scaly buds into which it retreats during the winter. If you think you can find a place for this gentle giant, refrain from planting until the spring so that it has an opportunity to develop a good root system before the winter.

Hosta ventricosa

Fish and other Livestock

Enlivening the pool with fish

A garden pool is not complete unless it has a complement of ornamental fish. Even if your main interest is plants, do not neglect this aspect of water gardening, for, apart from enlivening the pool with their antics, they are beneficial in controlling aquatic insect life such as mosquito larvae.

There are quite a number of different hardy ornamental fish suitable for the garden pool, but all have similar requirements and comparable stocking rates. The number of fish a pool will hold is a perpetual topic of discussion for which there are no hard and fast rules. However, through experience I have discovered that 15cm length of fish, inclusive of tail, for every 0.093 square metre of water surface, except in the very smallest pools, is the maximum that can be achieved without causing discomfort to the fish. In a newly established pool this ratio is undesirable, for most gardeners like to see their fish grow and also get quite a thrill if they happen to breed. Neither of which is likely to occur in a fully stocked environment.

Initial stocking of about a quarter of the maximum rate will allow the fish to develop naturally. At this juncture it should be noted that all ornamental fish grow in accordance with their surroundings. Thus a small goldfish which has been confined to a round glass bowl for several years will remain the same size, yet once liberated into a garden pool will almost certainly double its size within a season.

Another interesting fact to appreciate is that most fish consistently occupy one level of the water. Thus golden orfe will be found just beneath the surface of the water, goldfish and carp towards the middle zone, and green tench and catfish on the pool floor. Of course, all swim about freely and occupy one another's territory from time to time, but knowledge of their more usual habits enables a selection to be made so that all three zones are constantly inhabited. Although this should in no way alter the ratio of fish length to surface area.

May I also reinforce here the point that I made earlier, that fish must not be introduced to the pool until all the plants are well established.

Choosing your fish

Before venturing amongst the many varieties of ornamental fish that can be introduced to a garden pool, I feel that we ought to get clear what a healthy fish looks like. Healthy stock is of paramount importance whenever fish are introduced. A small diseased goldfish placed in a pool with established, vigorous, healthy specimens will quickly lead to disaster.

All fish that are in good health have stiff erect fins and bright eyes. Smaller sizes, especially, should not have any scales missing as these leave an opening for infection. They do on larger fish as well, but it is almost impossible to find an adult fish that is intact. If an otherwise healthy adult fish has a scale or two missing, dip it in a solution of malachite green before introducing it to the pool. This should go a long way towards preventing fungal disease gaining a hold.

Obviously any fish that are thought to be diseased or suffering from general malaise must be avoided. One or two species develop specific characteristics before their demise. Green tench turn from a lovely greyish olive-green to black and catfish behave similarly. Some carp suffer from a condition known as 'Big Head' in which the head seems over-large and the body narrow and pinched. Nobody is certain what causes this, although in some cases it could be fish tuberculosis, but whatever it is, death is swift. Those delightful little

Ornamental fish add the finishing touch to a garden pool.

dumpty fantails are prone to swim bladder disorders. So any that swim more or less permanently upside-down or in a crazed fashion should be regarded with suspicion.

Although it is not always possible, it is preferable to select your own fish. If this proves impractical, then place your requirements in the hands of a reliable supplier.

Mail order suppliers despatch fish in heavy gauge polythene bags with just sufficient water for them to maintain equilibrium, the remainder of the bag being blown up with oxygen and then placed in a stout cardboard carton. These are then despatched overnight by passenger train. On arrival remove the bag, and without unfastening, allow it to float on the surface of the pool. This enables the temperature of the warmer water within the bag to be equalised with that of the pool. After a short time the fish can be released into their new home. On a very hot day gently tip the fish into the pool without floating the bag, for the stifling effect of the hot sun can be more harmful than putting the fish into icy water.

Ornamental fish

There are many decorative fish from which to choose, but the goldfish is the regular favourite. Needing little introduction, this amiable character is fully hardy and comes in a range of colours that extends from white through yellow and orange to red.

Shubunkins are a transparent-scaled variety of goldfish in which almost every colour of the spectrum is represented. Blues, reds, oranges, white and yellow all appear, either alone or with one or all of the other colours, and in broad patches or spots. Strains which are of uniform colouration and which breed true to type have been given names and are much prized by the enthusiast. Those with a combination of blue

Blue shubunkin

Fantail goldfish

shades, like Cambridge Blue and Bristol Blue shubunkins, being particularly beautiful.

Apart from the diversity of colour offered by goldfish and shubunkins, there is also a wide range of forms. Comet long-tailed varieties for instance. These are of conventional body shape, perhaps somewhat slimmer, but with long flowing tails often as long as their bodies. They are very hardy and the bright red and golden-yellow selections are exceptional.

Fantails and veiltails have short rounded bodies and tripartite tails. They occur in a wide range of colours, but the group collectively

known as red and white fantails in which the fish are boldly splashed and marked with red and silver is generally the most popular and freely available. However, the calico fantails should not be overlooked, for these are the shubunkin form in which the body is marbled and stained with red, black, white or maroon on a powder-blue background. Most of the fancy goldfish with pendant spreading tails are, strictly speaking, fantails. The veiltail varieties differ only in having somewhat square and longer tails and high dorsal fins. These are really more graceful and slightly less hardy mutants of the fantail.

Some varieties also have bulbous or telescopic eyes. In all other respects they are identical to the typical fantail, red varieties being called red telescopes and multicoloured specimens being referred to as calico telescopes or calico moors. But the most impressive of all these variations is the black moor, a sleek, velvety-black fish with handsome tripartite tail and telescopic eyes.

Orandas have the appearance of a veiltail, but with curious strawberry-like growths on their heads, while lionheads have no dorsal fin and similar growths which suggest a lion's mane. But the most bizarre of all are the celestials. Long sleek fish with flattened heads and large upturned eyes.

Many other fancy varieties are kept by enthusiasts and bear names such as bubble-eye, toad head and pearl-scale. All beautiful and graceful creatures of exceptional merit, but sadly not robust enough to withstand the rough and tumble of garden pool life. As I intimated earlier, all comet long-tailed varieties are absolutely hardy, but the remainder need a depth of at least 45cm at one point in the pool if they are to overwinter successfully. However, the small risk involved in keeping these slightly less robust fancy varieties is greatly outweighed by the enormous pleasure they give.

Carp are absolutely hardy, and while a number like the mirror and crucian carp are only suitable for large ponds, the lovely Japanese Nishiki Koi is well suited to the garden pool. Koi occur in almost every colour imaginable and have shiny mirror scales which make them look strangely iridescent. Indeed, the Japanese word Nishiki means brocaded and is a very apt description.

Coloured carp generally grow larger than goldfish and differ

Common goldfish

Shubunkins

Black moor, an unusual variation of the goldfish.

technically in their fin structure, but more obviously in the presence of barbels at each side of their mouths. Although a wide colour range is obtainable amongst the mixed hybrids, the better fish are usually discovered within the myriad named varieties. These distinct forms mostly breed true to type and are available in striking hues. Unfortunately, they are all burdened with incomprehensible Japanese names, but generally speaking they are no more difficult to come to grips with than the latin names attached to plants. Sanke is white with red and black markings; Shiro-ogen white; Ki-ogen yellow and Bekko tortoise-shell.

The closely related Higoi carp can also be wholeheartedly recommended. This is just another variety of coloured carp which in technical circles is joined with the Nishiki Koi. However, to the layman it is quite distinct, being easily recognisable with its slightly depressed head, strong lips and conspicuous pendant barbels. It is a uniform shade of salmon or orange-pink and popularly known as the Chinese red carp.

The golden orfe is of similar colouration, but with a silvery belly and occasional splashes of black on the head. It is a slender, fast swimming, shoal fish which generally lives just beneath the surface of the water, where on warm summer evenings it may be observed leaping for flies. This handsome fish enjoys well-oxygenated water, never being happier than when frolicking in the spray of a fountain or the outfall of a cascade. Remember this when buying golden orfe. Never purchase them on a hot day when oxygen is rapidly depleted or in larger sizes which are difficult to move. The same applies to its more sombre cousin the silver orfe.

Rudd are a little more resilient

Golden orfe

Silver rudd

and can be moved quite easily in the larger sizes. Like orfe they tend to shoal together and keep reasonably near the surface of the water. They are not quite so attractive, the ordinary silvery variety only being noted for its reddish fins and the golden kind having a golden metallic lustre rather than being a pure self-colour. In the large pool with plenty of submerged plant growth rudd breed quite freely if left to their own devices.

The same cannot be said for the bitterling, for this lively little fish deposits its eggs in the mantle cavity of a living painters' mussel. Here the eggs are incubated and hatch, the tiny fry only leaving the shelter of their host when large enough to fend for themselves.

The bitterling is a small attractive fish, having the appearance of a tiny carp, but with a lustrous metallic sheen which in the male is further enhanced during spring and early summer by the appearance of blue and purple breeding colours. It is a very active little fellow and adds considerable life to the pool, but, unfortunately, seldom lives for more than three or four years and so needs replacing periodically.

The minnow is a similar proposition and a welcome addition to the garden pool when clean and healthy stock can be obtained. Although in its natural haunts it is a fish of shallow, fast moving streams, it adapts well to the more placid life of the garden pool, particularly when it can leap and play in the gentle spray of a fountain. Of a gregarious nature, the minnow needs introducing in quantity if it is to be happy and create an effect.

For much of the year minnows are a silvery colour, but with the first warm spring sunshine the males develop their characteristic breeding colours. These are variable, the fish usually become very dark, almost black, with glowing red bellies and conspicuous crimson markings at the corners of the mouths. Their flanks are sprinkled with dark spots and their heads with large nuptial turbucles.

Roach will also successfully adapt to pond life, and while they may not be the most decorative of coldwater fish they find a place in the large and medium sized pool. They are slim, deep-bodied fish of a steely-grey colour with bright red irises to the eyes. A characteristic which distinguishes them clearly from the closely allied dace.

Dace are not quite so accommodating as roach, for like orfe, they enjoy well-oxygenated water. They are also shoal fish and should be introduced in reasonable numbers if they are to be happy. Although they are very active and doubtless useful in the larger pool, where strict limits upon the fish population are imposed the more colourful golden orfe are preferable.

Many other species can be kept happily and successfully with those just mentioned. These include a number of native species like the Prussian carp, gudgeon and leather carp. However, few of these are particularly decorative and are only indulged in by the serious fish keeper. But this line of thought leads me to one extremely important point when dealing with native fish. Never introduce stock captured in the wild. The chances are that these

Green tench, a scavenging fish.

will be diseased, and although possibly not showing any visible signs owing to their inherent resistance, once introduced to the relatively sterile environment of a garden pool any infection will spread like wildfire and decimate the domestic population.

Scavenging fish

Most pool owners want at least a couple of scavenging fish in their pool, for these will clear up uneaten goldfish food and also dispose of gnat larvae and other undesirable creatures. Unfortunately, many newcomers believe that scavenging fish will be the magical cure that will ensure clear water, devouring green suspended algae and blanket-weed as well as all the mulm that naturally occurs on a pool floor. This popular misconception is unfortunate, for it tends to lead the pool owner to believe that the pool can be left to its own devices once stocked, and that the scavengers will take care of any problems that arise. They then tend to be lazy about maintaining a natural balance of plant life which is really the magical cure.

Green tench are the most popular scavenging fish. These have short broad bodies and distinctive tapering heads. In common with all the other so-called scavengers, they

inhabit the murky depths of the pool and are only rarely seen. Therefore, little would seem to be gained by introducing its orange-yellow variety, the golden tench, an often recommended addition or substitute for the ordinary green kind. As this is quite an expensive character and seldom visible its use should be restricted to the coldwater aquarium.

The same might be said for the various coldwater catfish, for although they have been traditionally sold as scavenging fish, they are really not suitable. There are three different hardy catfish sold by dealers in this country. The horned pout, the brown bullhead and the German wels or waller. All look superficially alike, with slender, slippery, grey, black or brown bodies, broad heads and long barbels or whiskers. In their juvenile stage there may be something to be said for including them, for they feed voraciously upon all manner of aquatic insect life. However, as they mature their tastes alter and they then prey upon fry and other small fishes.

Snails and mussels

Snails are useful for devouring filamentous algae and rotting vegetation. But is is important to get the right species as some will do considerable damage to plant life if given the opportunity.

The only species that can be unreservedly recommended is the ramshorn snail, a pleasant fellow with a flattened shell like a catherine wheel which the creature carries in an upright position on its back. The shell is deep brown, or sometimes black, while the snail within may be red, white or more usually black.

Some nurserymen mistakenly sell the freshwater whelk as a pond snail, and while it is true that it will feed upon algae, it much prefers to chew the broad verdant pads of waterlilies. This is an easily recognised species with a tall, pointed and spiralled shell which houses a greyish snail.

A number of other species are not infrequently offered for sale, amongst them the diminutive ear pond snail and the wandering pond snail. Both look superficially like the freshwater whelk, but are considerably smaller, the ear pond snail being further distinguished by an extra large aperture. Neither is generally destructive to plant life, but owing to their small size must be introduced in greater numbers if they are to be effective.

There are no hard and fast rules as to the number of snails necessary for a particular volume of water, although there is little sense in introducing fewer than a dozen to the average pool. With algae-eating species the population will quite naturally rise and fall with the availability of food. Thus the greener the pool the more snails it will support. Likewise, the more abundant the aquatic plant life, the greater the population of undesirable snails will become.

When undesirable species have been accidentally introduced into a pool they can be captured with some degree of success by floating a fresh lettuce leaf on the surface of the water. Snails will congregate beneath this and can then be removed and discarded. If a fresh leaf is introduced daily, surprising numbers of snails can be captured over the period of a week or two.

It is, of course, preferable not to introduce undesirable species in the first place. But apart from misguidedly buying the wrong kind, they are often accidentally introduced as eggs on the feet of birds bathing in the shallows. Or more frequently still on freshly purchased plants. All new plants should be carefully inspected before placing in the pool and any snail eggs removed. It is not necessary to discard those that appear in a flat pad of jelly as these belong to the desirable ramshorn snail. However, any that appear in a cylinder of clear jelly should be removed, as they are likely to have been produced by the troublesome species.

Mussels can be useful inhabitants of a pool, but a prerequisite for success is a natural floor or a good accumulation of mulm in which they can shuffle. A clean pool with well scrubbed walls and floor will quickly bring about their demise. The putrefying remains of just a couple of mussels will cause considerable pollution.

There are two species of mussel popularly used. The swan mussel, which has an oval brownish-green shell with a white fleshy body and the painters' mussel, a smaller kind with a yellowish-green shell marked with brown. Both filter water and retain minute suspended aquatic life assisting with the clarification of water and thus making a significant contribution to the well-being of the pool.

Other livestock

Before departing from fish and other livestock I must just make a mention of native creatures which may enter the pool of their own accord. Pool owners often feel concern if they discover frogs, toads, or newts in their pool. I have even heard of some pool owners removing the poor creatures and destroying them in case they were preying upon fish.

Generally speaking, all native amphibians are welcome additions to the pool community, feeding exclusively upon insect life and not interfering at all with the fish, snails or plants, nor affecting the balance of the pool in any way. Indeed, the garden pool is the last retreat for many of our amphibians, for their natural habitats have been rapidly depleted by land drainage and modern farming techniques.

Of course, most amphibians only spend their breeding life in the water, the rest of the time scampering about the poolside and eventually hibernating in some secluded corner. Their tadpoles are an excellent live fish food and a constant source of amusement. The only problem that may occur with a frog in the pond is the attachment of a solitary male to a fish. This only occurs when there is no female present, the frog clasping the fish around the gills in typical breeding stance and causing considerable damage.

Other creatures which are some-times introduced to the water garden are the water tortoises or pond terrapins. There are five different species of these lumbering reptiles which are hardy in Great Britain, but only the European pond tortoise and Spanish terrapin are at all common.

These require a considerable amount of space if they are not to create havoc amongst the waterside plants. They are also carnivorous, and while usually directing their attentions towards leeches, worms and beetles they are not adverse to taking a small fish or two.

Managing the Water Garden

The pool in spring

The spring is traditionally the time for introducing new aquatic plants to the pool. They then have all summer to become established, and if planted at this time will usually provide a display the first season.

Not only are there replacements to be made for occasional losses sustained during the winter, but a number of subjects will need dividing and replanting if they are to retain their vigour and keep within bounds. I like to lift and divide marginal plants in alternate years. However, it is not desirable to divide all the plants at one time as this leads to what one might call fat years and lean years – the newly replanted material looking rather sparse early on and then the entire pool appearing overcrowded. It is much more sensible to lift and divide half of the plants each year.

Waterlilies do not need attention so often. The third year of their establishment being an appropriate time to divide vigorous varieties, while some of the more restrained kinds will last for four or five years without attention. The need for division will be apparent in any case if the plants make a preponderance of small leafy growth in the centre of the clump. Especially if this is accompanied by

diminishing flower size.

Submerged plants can often be left for a number of years without attention, although the stringy winter growth of species like *Lagarosiphon major* should be removed each spring to allow fresh growth to break from the bottom. If a basket of oxygenating subjects is not growing very well it is a good idea to shake out the soil and replant healthy young cuttings in fresh compost.

When dividing marginal plants treat them like herbaceous perennials. Tough rootstocks being separated by inserting two hand forks back to back and levering the plant apart. I like to replant material from the outer edge of the clump as this if full of the vigour of youth.

Waterlilies can be treated similarly, except that in most cases they will need to be separated with a knife and, therefore, care should be taken to see that any wounds are dressed with powdered charcoal to prevent infection.

On lifting a healthy mature waterlily the rootstock will be seen to consist of a main rhizome, which was the one originally planted, together with a number of side branches. It is these side growths that should be retained as they are young and vigorous, the original

rootstock being discarded. Each severed branch will produce a plant providing that it has a healthy terminal shoot.

It may be appropriate at this juncture to briefly discuss the propagation of aquatic plants. Although few gardeners will envisage growing more than one or two kinds, it is useful to know how they are increased.

By and large marginal plants are increased by division, although some of the more vigorous kinds like *Mentha aquatica* and *Veronica beccabunga* are easily reproduced from short stem cuttings pushed into a pot of wet mud. *Butomus umbellatus* produces large quantities of tiny bulbils along its rootstock. These can be removed and planted in a seed tray of wet mud until large enough to reintroduce to the pool.

Seed finds a place in the propagation of aquatics, but it must be sown fresh and in most cases not allowed to dry out. The seed of *Pontederia cordata* must be sown when still green if it is to germinate satisfactorily, while that of *Aponogeton distachyus* should only briefly leave the water. Calla, lysichitum and orontium seed must be well ripened before sowing and preferably put in before the winter, while that of *Myosotis scorpioides* can

A plant lover's pool illustrating the wide variety of material available for a modern water garden.

be sown at any time.

Waterlilies do not set seed freely and apart from *Nymphaea tetragona* and the closely allied *N.pygmaea alba*, are not normally increased in this manner. These two are quite readily reproduced this way, although once again the seed should not be allowed to dry out. Sown in pans of wet mud and covered with a little water they germinate freely, but are vulnerable to the choking growth of filamentous algae. So they need constant attention. As they grow stronger they can be potted and stood in an aquarium or bucket of water until large enough to be safely planted out.

This is not the most usual method of propagation, for waterlilies are commonly increased from eyes in the spring. These eyes occur with varying frequency along the rhizomes of mature plants. In some cases they are latent and look like those of a potato tuber, whereas others appear as smaller versions of the main growing point. Yet a third kind, common in *Nymphaea tuberosa* and its varieties, takes the form of brittle rounded nodules.

All are treated in the same manner irrespective of their appearance, being removed from the rootstock with a sharp knife. The wounds on both eye and rhizome being dusted with powdered charcoal. The eyes are potted into small pots in a heavy loam soil and placed in a shallow container with water just over their rims. They are then stood in a greenhouse or on the window-sill.

After three or four weeks, growth will have started and the tiny leaf stems will be lengthening. At this time the water level should be gradually raised until the leaves are floating with their stems fully extended. As further growth is made the level should be raised and the plants progressively potted until

sufficiently robust to withstand the rigours of pond life.

Replanting and propagating are normal spring activities, but an equally important, and yet often overlooked, task is feeding. Once planted, most gardeners tend to think that aquatic plants will look after themselves. While this is broadly speaking true, far better results can be obtained by the judicious use of fertilisers. But applying fertilisers is not as easy as it sounds where a pool is concerned. Obviously one must consider the livestock, and it is well known that many fertilisers are toxic to fish and snails. Even 'safe' fertilisers must be used with care, for the majority will drastically increase the level of mineral salts in the water and thus create a dense green algal bloom.

Fortunately, manufacturers have come up with a system which curtails both of these problems, for it is now possible to buy small perforated plastic sachets of slow release fertiliser which can be pushed into the soil beside a waterlily or marginal plant and provide it with nourishment. The more traditional method of achieving the same end is by making what are known as bonemeal 'pills'. These consist of balls of wet clay soil which are mixed with coarse bonemeal and then pushed into the compost beside each aquatic plant. The frequency with which this needs to be done is variable and depends upon the condition of the individual plant. However, I would think that the annual treatment of most subjects would be sufficient.

Caring for the pool in summer

The pool needs very little attention during the summer months if it is well balanced. The plants should be flourishing and the fish gliding about happily. Warm weather causes evaporation and this should be

corrected regularly. Rain water is ideal for topping up the pool, but tap water is a good second best. The only problem this may create is a temporary green haze as suspended algae take advantage of the abundance of fresh mineral salts that has been added. This is only a minor irritation. Nothing compared with the trouble a plastic pool liner will give if an area between soil and water level is continually exposed to the sun. In these circumstances the pool liner becomes bleached, brittle and quickly breaks up.

Fish capture our attention more during the summer than at any other time of the year. And what delightful creatures they are! Especially if you have the time and patience to feed them regularly. It is not that they are likely to need anything if the pool is well balanced, for there is always an abundance of insect life available. It is just that, like us, they will not work if they do not have to, and taking food from the human hand is far simpler than hunting elusive worms and mosquito larvae.

It is correct that if one feeds ornamental fish at the same place in the pool each day, after a short period of time they will rush to that spot merely at the sound of a footfall or when a shadow is cast across the water. This can lead to endless fun, for some species become so thrilled with the arrangement that they will take particles of food from your fingers.

The kind of food offered, the quantity, and the frequency with which it is given are perpetual topics of conversation amongst fish fanciers. In the summer feeding can take place every other day, sufficient being given to keep the fish occupied for about twenty minutes. Any that remains uneaten being netted off and the quantity reduced by that amount the next feeding time. Of course, feeding should be directly related to the activity of the fish, which in the summer is heightened by the warmer weather. Therefore during spring, and again in the autumn, it will be discovered that fish will only eat normally on bright sunny days, and, therefore, should be treated accordingly.

There is a wide variety of staple foods to choose from and all have their advocates. These basically take three different forms. The conventional or crumb form in a mixture of colours and looking very much like biscuit meal. Flaked foods. which take the form of thin tissues of flake-like breakfast cereal, and the floating pellet variety, which are brownish or grey in colour and of similar appearance to the concentrated pellets on which farmers feed poultry and rabbits.

The traditional biscuit or crumb form has little to commend it except price, for it is much cheaper than other kinds. Unfortunately, it sinks rather quickly and the fish tend to miss it, so its purchase in preference to other varieties is a dubious economy.

Both flaked and pelleted fish foods float for a considerable time, but on a blustery day the flaked ones are quickly blown away, so that leaves us with pellets. The only black mark that I can place against them is their size. Although at least one enterprising manufacturer has introduced a pelleted food in mixed sizes. However, most distribute pellets of a large uniform size which are frustrating for smaller fish who have to suck continuously at them to gain any nourishment and also run the risk of being choked.

Apart from staple diets there are many other varieties of fish food which can be fed with advantage. Dried flies, shredded shrimp and daphnia are amongst the most popular, although freeze dried foods

like mosquito larvae and tubifex worms are making advances. All are nutritious, but must not be fed continuously. Rather should they be used sparingly to add occasional variety to what must be very dull fare.

Live foods are much relished, but like the dry kinds must be fed only occasionally. Daphnia and tubifex worms are the favourites, daphnia being especially useful as they can be set up in a self-perpetuating culture at home. Add a couple of centimetres of soil to a tub of rain water. This will quickly turn green with algae. Then introduce a small net of daphnia. This feeds on the algae and breeds in the murky depths at an amazing rate. Sufficient during warm sunny weather to provide a pool full of fish with two decent meals each week.

The summer is also the time when pond fish breed. And what headaches they seem to cause the new pond owner. Unnecessary, of course, but understandable if one has no idea of what is going on.

To start from the beginning, we will assume that the pool owner would like to breed a few fish. Thus allowing those who have no intention of following this pursuit, and who only get involved accidentally through the will of Nature, to extract any useful information. So we start with selecting breeding pairs of fish on the understanding that with the exception of catfish, which belong to a different group, and bitterling, which have their own way of doing things, all are of the carp family and perform in a very similar manner.

Adult fish all look the same to the untrained eye, but if we take goldfish as an example, we will see that some are slim and pencil-like, while others are rather dumpy and, if viewed from above, more or less oval in outline. The chunky ones are

female and the more slender ones male. In spring and summer this can be further verified by looking at the heads, and more particularly the gill plates, of suspected males for these should be covered in white pimples or nuptial turbucles. The occurrence of these varies considerably from fish to fish and species to species.

Breeding is not so much geared to age as size. Thus any young goldfish in excess of 8cm in length is capable of reproducing. But only during the spring and summer, the frequency of spawning being directly related to the temperature of the water. When several fish are seen chasing around the pool and brushing against one another they are almost certainly spawning. I will not go into the technicalities of fish breeding, but what basically happens is that fertilised spawn is wrapped around submerged plant life, the tiny fish quickly emerging and clinging to leaves and stems. After two or three weeks, those that have survived being eaten by their elders, will be seen swimming around the pool. They look like miniature versions of their parents and may be either transparent or bronze, but with the passage of time attaining their proper hues.

No special attention is needed for adults or fry. However, if you seriously wish to keep a few home-bred fish, ensure their safety in early life. Collect some submerged plant with spawn attached as soon as possible after it is deposited. Then put this in a bucket containing water from the pond and most of the fry will develop unhindered. As there will be little food available to them they should be fed on a baby fish food, which is easily obtainable from any pet shop, or tiny pieces of egg yolk.

Preparing for the winter
It is surprising how many gardeners

neglect their pools once the last waterlily blossom has faded. The dull wet days of autumn descend and they take to their firesides thinking that like on the vegetable patch, nothing is happening in the pool. This is regrettable, for more trouble can ensue from neglecting a pool in the autumn than at any other time of the year.

The first problem to be tackled is that of falling leaves from surrounding trees. Even a small accumulation in the bottom of the pool can be dangerous, particularly if like horse-chestnut, they are toxic as well. A fine mesh net placed across the pool is absolutely essential until the trees are bare.

Marginal plants must be cleaned up once the frost has turned the foliage brown. Reduce them by about two-thirds of their height. Never cut them below water level, for some aquatics have hollow stems and will actually die from drowning. However, it is important that they are all tidied up so that they do not become a winter refuge for insect pests.

Waterlilies need no winter preparation as they are perfectly hardy and die down naturally without fuss. We only need feel concern for pygmy varieties in a rock pool or sink, as these can be damaged by severe weather. The best method of protection is to drain the water off and then give the waterlilies a liberal covering of straw. They survive well like this and can easily be started into growth again in the spring by the addition of water.

Floating plants disappear one by one as the days shorten, retreating into winter buds or turions which fall to the pool floor where they remain until the spring sunshine warms the water again. As I mentioned when describing various floating plants earlier in the book, it is useful to collect some of the over-wintering buds and keep them in jars of water with a little soil in the bottom. If stood in a light frost-free place they start into growth much sooner and are an invaluable aid in the battle against algae. By being well advanced they provide surface shade during early spring, a good few weeks before those that are resting naturally on the pool floor appear.

Fish should be prepared for the winter by judicious feeding with daphnia, ant eggs and other delicacies on days when the weather is warm and bright and they are seen to be active. Precautions for their winter welfare should be taken at this time with the introduction of a pool heater.

The pool in winter
The pool in winter is an inhospitable place and often causes concern to the newcomer to water gardening. Worries about the safety of the fish are quite natural, but providing sensible precautions are taken the majority will come to no harm.

Most decorative coldwater fish are extremely hardy. During the winter their metabolism slows down much in the same way as a tree becomes dormant. Therefore, being inactive they feed less. So please refrain from feeding them at all during the winter. Uneaten fish food will just fall to the floor of the pool and decompose. This semi-dormant state is particularly valuable to fish, enabling them to be frozen more or less solid in ice for a few days without apparently coming to any harm. In fact, a prolonged period with a layer of ice over the surface of the pool is likely to cause more casualties owing to the build-up of obnoxious gases beneath.

In a well-maintained pool the problem of gases is not so acute as there is much less organic debris to decay. But once a layer of ice has formed there is no way of knowing exactly what is going on beneath and it is a wise precaution to keep at least a small area free from ice.

The simplest method of doing this is by installing a pool heater. This consists of a heated brass rod with a polystyrene float which can be connected to the electrical supply which operates the pump. Even in severe frosts this will create a small ice-free area. If electricity is not close at hand, the safest way of obtaining a similar effect is by standing a pan of boiling water on the ice and allowing it to melt through. Never strike the ice with a heavy instrument as this will concuss and often kill the fish.

A carefully planted pool showing the healthy balance that comes with maturity.

Common Pool Problems

Pests of water plants

Probably the most trouble-some pest of aquatic plants is the waterlily aphis, for not only does it attack nymphaeas, but all manner of succulent marginals as well. Looking very much like the notorious black bean aphis, this little pest breeds at a prodigious rate, smothering leaves, stems and flowers and causing widespread disfigurement.

The breeding habits and complicated life cycle of this pest are worth studying. However, it is sufficient to say here that reproduction takes place continuously on the host plants during the summer months, followed by mass migration to nearby plum and cherry trees during early autumn. Here eggs are deposited on the boughs where they over-winter, the emerging generation next spring returning to the water plants.

Obviously control of any insect infestation in a pool which is stocked with fish is likely to be difficult. All that can be recommended is washing the pests into the pool with a strong jet of clear water and hope that the fish will clear them up. Some will doubtless climb back onto the foliage, but if the process is repeated regularly they will be kept under control.

Spraying neighbouring plum and cherry trees with a winter tar oil wash will considerably reduce the over-wintering population. It also follows that when planning a pool, consideration should be given to the placing of trees of this family within the surrounding garden. Never, for instance, use one of the weeping flowering cherries at the poolside. Although it may well look delightful, it will be impossible to keep aphis-free.

Waterlily beetles can also be troublesome, but are fortunately only of local occurrence. The small dark brown beetles and shiny black larvae will be found on both foliage and flowers of waterlilies where the latter strips them of epidermal tissue. This results in infection and subsequent decay.

Again, forcibly spraying with clear water will dislodge the pests, but it is equally important to remove the dead remains of poolside plants during the autumn as it is here that waterlily beetles take refuge during the winter.

Both the beautiful china mark moth and brown china mark moth can cause considerable damage to aquatic plants. The little brownish and orange moths look inoffensive enough, which indeed they are. It is their caterpillars that cause all the trouble. These cut and shred the foliage, those of the beautiful china mark moth even having the audacity to burrow into the stems as well. Not content with cutting up foliage, they then proceed to stick pieces together and form a shelter in which they can live in comparative safety.

Even if it were possible to spray with insecticide they would be fairly secure. The only method of control that is effective is handpicking. This is a long and tedious business, especially if the infestation is severe. Under such circumstances it is better to remove the foliage from all deep water aquatics and net off all pieces of floating plant debris. Hopefully most of the larvae will be removed and the plants can make fresh healthy growth from the base.

Caddis flies have larvae which live in a similar manner, constructing shelters from all sorts of pond debris and in this relative safety feeding on all kinds of aquatic plants. There is very little chance of effecting a control, either manual or chemical, for apart from being sturdily built their shelters are well camouflaged. Fortunately, fish consider such larvae a delicacy and providing the pool is adequately stocked they should cause very little trouble.

False leaf-mining midge sometimes makes an appearance in the pool and when it does the effect can be devastating. The tiny larvae attack the floating foliage of deep water aquatics, eating a narrow tracery of lines all over the surface. These usually remain unnoticed until the damaged parts become infected and the entire leaf rots and collapses. This can be particularly serious for less vigorous waterlilies. Forcible spraying of the foliage immediately damage is noticed will control the pest, but by this time the foliage is unlikely to recover.

Aquatic plant diseases

Fortunately, few diseases affect water plants, but those that do are particularly destructive and difficult to control.

Leaf spots are the most frequent assailants with two distinct species attacking the foliage of waterlilies, but causing similar damage. This appears in the form of dark patches on or around the edges of the leaves, which eventually rot through and lead to the collapse of the foliage. Both are very infectious and spread through a pond like wildfire, so immediately trouble is spotted the infected plants should be removed and destroyed. Spraying with a weak solution of Bordeaux mixture in the absence of fish will contain the disease, but unless a rare or special variety is infected, treatment is not worthwhile.

With waterlily root rot the same applies. In fact, nothing can be done to arrest this disease once it takes a hold, but the waterlilies that remain in the pool can be protected by impregnating the water with copper sulphate. A small quantity of crystals being tied up in a muslin bag and dragged through the water until dissolved. All fish must be removed before doing this as copper sulphate is toxic. Personally I would never attempt such treatment in an ordinary garden pool. It is far better to remove and destroy the waterlilies and do without them for a season rather than risk the lives of the fish.

Waterlily root rot is not difficult to diagnose, for affected plants have leaf and flower stems which become soft and blackened, and evil-smelling roots which turn gelatinous. An altogether unsavoury disease which is usually introduced with freshly purchased plants. So never plant a waterlily that has a soft or blackened area on its rootstock. Even if it turns out not to be root rot it is better to be safe than sorry.

When the pool turns cloudy

I am not going to propose any magical cure-all for a dirty or green pond, rather am I going to suggest the reasons for it and leave the pool owner to take what action he sees fit. To put not too fine a point on its, except in its initial stages of establishment, the degree of un-cleanliness of a pool reflects to a considerable extent the degree of mismanagement by its owner. I do not mean to be harsh, but having dealt with this particular problem from pool owners over a number of years, I find that the greatest obstacle to putting matters right is the questioner's belief that he cannot possibly have done anything wrong, and that there is a special chemical that can be added to the water which will give instant clarity. If the pool owner is prepared to humble himself and read on, then he is well on the way to correcting the trouble.

There are three main kinds of cloudy water. Green water, which is caused by suspended algae; muddy water, which is brought about by the distribution of soil particles; and evil-smelling milky water which is a sure sign that something is decaying on the pool floor.

Let us look at the last condition first. This is directly attributable to decaying organic matter within the pool and is extremely serious, causing rapid oxygen depletion and loss of fish. Only by emptying the pool and removing the offending pollutant can this condition be cured. In a small pool the occasional loss of a sizable fish and its subsequent decomposition may cause the trouble, but more often than not it is due to the accumulation of dead leaves from surrounding trees. Netting the pool at leaf fall will prevent the trouble recurring.

Dirty or muddy water might not be so easy to cure. Especially if the pool is natural or the plants have been planted directly on to the marginal shelves or the pool floor. Fish stirring up mud in their search for insect larvae are the usual culprits, tench and carp being particularly troublesome.

The only way to cure such a problem is to ensure that all exposed areas of soil are covered with a generous layer of pea shingle. This prevents the fish from nosing about and stirring up the soil, yet allows them to withdraw delicacies such as gnat larvae. When the plants are grown in baskets this is easily done, but if they have been planted directly into soil the entire pool must be emptied before the gravel can be distributed.

If we now turn to green water we find the commonest and most frustrating problem the pool owner encounters. As suggested earlier, green water is brought about basically by bad management. Temporary opaqueness in a pool where the plants have not become established is quite normal and eventually corrects itself. There may also be a green algal bloom in the water during the first warm days of spring owing to the aquatic plants not having surged into growth. But permanently green water needs more plants.

I am not going to rewrite the theory of natural balance here, but it is essential to have sufficient submerged oxygenating plants to compete with the algae for mineral salts. About a third of the surface area must also be covered by floating foliage in order to reduce the amount of direct sunlight falling beneath the water and thus make life intolerable for slimes and algae. This is the only way to permanent clarity.

Algaecides are useful in achieving a balance, but are not a substitute for it. I am generally against the widespread use of chemicals in horticulture, but there is a case for using them in a newly established pool to kill off rapidly growing green algae. The algae reduce the intensity of sunlight beneath the water and, therefore, the speed of growth of the all important submerged plants. The same applies to a mature green pond where additional submerged plants are being introduced. Plunging containers full of oxygenating plants into murky green water will eventually effect a cure, but by destroying the algae chemically at the outset the plants will get a much better start and soon take control of the situation.

Common fish disorders

The pests and diseases that affect decorative fish are legion. Indeed, if we look at the diversity of ills that can befall a fish it is surprising that any have survived. Put into perspective though, they are dangers with which we should concern ourselves, but not serious threats if a good standard of pool hygiene is maintained and all new additions to the pool are carefully vetted.

Describing all the ailments that might befall fish in a garden pool

A mass of colour in and around the pool need not detract from the reflective qualities of the water.

would not only be tedious, but extremely depressing. So what I will do now is mention those that are likely to be encountered, together with early warning signs that something might be wrong. Correct treatment at an early stage will save fish from all diseases, except fish tuberculosis, and can help considerably when they have been attacked by insect predators.

Undoubtedly the most common problem the pool owner will have to contend with is fungus in all its various forms. This manifests itself as a white cotton wool-like growth which is usually a secondary infection on open wounds, although fish run down after the winter may develop it in patches on seemingly healthy parts of their bodies.

If treated as soon as noticed

fungus is not a serious malady. But if allowed to continue unchecked, is a slow killer which will gradually spread through a pond. Dipping affected fish regularly in a sea salt solution over a period of time usually brings about a cure, but modern fungus cures based on methylene blue and malachite green used in the same way result in a much speedier recovery.

Malachite green can also be used to cure that other unpleasant fish ailment, fin rot. Its popular name describes precisely what this bacteria does. Destroying fins and tails, and if not treated promptly, eating into the body of the fish as well and causing an extremely unpleasant death.

White spot disease is caused by a group of single celled creatures called protozoa which for part of their life cycle become embedded in the flesh of a fish. On their departure they leave deep pock marks which are open to infection by fungal diseases. Not only that, but the cycle is recurring and if left unchecked the parasites will re-infest the fish in ever increasing numbers until it eventually becomes weakened and dies.

At the stage in which the parasite is embedded in the fish it is fairly safe. However, once it bores its way through the skin and becomes free-swimming it is extremely vulnerable and can be easily killed by methylene blue or else quinine salts such as quinine hydrochloride and quinine sulphate. Such treatment can only be provided for fish in small volumes of water and is both impractical and undesirable to attempt in the open pool. The best way of ridding a pool of the parasites is to leave it devoid of fish for six weeks. During that period of time all free-swimming parasites have to find a host or perish.

Several pests attack fish, some of which are hideous in their cruelty.

The anchor worm, for instance, not strictly speaking a worm, but a brutal crustacean. This has a slender tube-like body less than 1cm long with a horrible barbed head which it imbeds in the flesh of its host. During its murderous feast lesions and unsightly tumours appear which eventually become infected with fungus, leading to the eventual death of the fish. Affected fish must be captured and held in a net while the anchor worm is dabbed with a solution of potassium permanganate or domestic paraffin. This kills the creature, which can then be withdrawn with tweezers and the open wound treated with a mild household disinfectant.

Fish lice perform in a similar manner, clinging to the body of the fish, especially in and around the gills. They are strange creatures with almost transparent flattened bodies and gruesome feelers with which they attach themselves to their host. Paraffin dabbed on their bodies dislodges them, but it is important to dip the fish in a malachite green solution before returning them to the pond as some of the fleshy tissue will have doubtless been damaged.

Leeches sometimes attack fish, although the majority of species prey upon snails. Dragonfly larvae can also cause trouble, as well as great diving beetles and water scorpions. None of these can be regarded as a serious threat though, for they will only attack an occasional fish and do not warrant any control measures. Beetles, leeches and scorpions are all part of pond life and we should accept them as such. A lost fish now and then is a small price to pay for the added interest these creatures can give a water garden. And after all it is just Nature's way of ensuring survival and maintaining a balance between the various life forms.

Before leaving the problems that might afflict fish, it is perhaps appropriate for me to mention the most humane method of killing an ailing fish. As will have been appreciated, most disorders can be treated with a reasonable amount of success if spotted early enough. However, some cases will have gone too far before they are discovered and on certain occasions the treatment may appear to cause extreme discomfort with only a slight chance of recovery. In these cases, and when a fish is carrying a highly contagious disease, it is best destroyed.

The fish to be disposed of should be taken in a dry cloth and then dashed smartly against a hard surface such as a concrete path. Death will be instantaneous.

Coping with the heron

Apart from all the problems that may occur within the pool, there are those that may quite unexpectedly come from outside. Of these the heron is likely to be the most troublesome.

It is well known that herons wade into the water and stand waiting for their unsuspecting prey. So small mesh netting can be spread out across the pool to stop their antics. Unfortunately, this not only looks unsightly, but causes all kinds of problems with the plants growing through it and eventually becomes an awful tangle.

The best deterrent I have found is a row of short pieces of cane, no more than 10cm high, placed at regular intervals around the perimeter of the pool. Attached to these is a strong black thread or fishing line. When the heron advances towards the pool his legs come in contact with the thread and he will go no further. After two or three sorties he will almost invariably skulk away.

Glossary

Recommended Waterlilies
All flower intermittently from June–September

NAME	COLOUR	MINIMUM DEPTH OF WATER	SPECIAL FEATURES
'Arc-en-Ciel'	Pale pink	45cm	Multi-coloured foliage
'Attraction'	Garnet red	75cm	Free-flowering
'Aurora'	Chameleon	30cm	Mottled foliage
candida	White	35cm	Very hardy
caroliniana	Pink	35cm	Fragrant
caroliniana 'Nivea'	White	35cm	Fragrant
caroliniana 'Perfecta'	Pale pink	35cm	Fragrant
caroliniana 'Rosea'	Rose pink	35cm	Fragrant
'Charles de Meurville'	Deep plum streaked white	75cm	Vigorous and free flowering
'Escarboucle'	Deep crimson	75cm	The best red
'Gloire de Temple-sur-Lot'	Pink	60cm	Fully double blossoms
'Gonnère'	White	60cm	Double snowball-like flowers
'Graziella'	Chameleon	30cm	Mottled foliage
'Hal Miller'	Creamy white	55cm	Blossoms of outstanding quality
'Hyperion'	Deep amaranth	15cm	Scarce, but very choice
'Indiana'	Chameleon	30cm	Mottled foliage
'James Brydon'	Dark red	75cm	Paeony-shaped blossoms
laydekeri 'Alba'	White	45cm	Fragrant
laydekeri 'Fulgens'	Crimson	45cm	Very free-flowering
laydekeri 'Lilacea'	Soft pink	45cm	Fragrant
laydekeri 'Purpurata'	Rich red	45cm	Bright orange stamens
marliacea 'Albida'	White	50cm	Free-flowering
marliacea 'Carnea'	Flesh pink	60cm	Vanilla fragrance
marliacea 'Chromatella'	Canary yellow	50cm	Mottled foliage
marliacea 'Flammea'	Fiery red	60cm	Mottled foliage
marliacea 'Ignea'	Crimson	60cm	Tulip-shaped
'Maurice Laydeker'	Deep red	20cm	Blossoms of exceptional texture
'Moorei'	Yellow	30cm	Spotted green leaves
odorata	White	45cm	Fragrant
odorata minor	White	20cm	Fragrant
odorata pumila	White	20cm	Fragrant
odorata rosea	Pink	45cm	Fragrant
odorata rubra	Crimson	45cm	Fragrant
odorata 'Firecrest'	Pink	50cm	Fragrant red-tipped stamens
odorata 'Helen Fowler'	Deep rose	75cm	Fragrant
odorata 'Luciana'	Deep rose	50cm	Fragrant
odorata 'Suavissima'	Rose pink	50cm	Richly fragrant
odorata 'Sulphurea'	Canary yellow	50cm	Fragrant, mottled foliage
odorata 'William B. Shaw'	Creamy pink	50cm	Fragrant
'Pearl of the Pool'	Bright pink	55cm	Double flowers
pygmaea alba	White	15cm	The best pygmy white
pygmaea 'Helvola'	Canary yellow	15cm	Mottled foliage
pygmaea 'Rubis'	Red	15cm	Large flowers
pygmaea 'Rubra'	Red	15cm	The best pygmy red
'René Gerard'	Rose splashed red	55cm	Free-flowering
'Rose Arey'	Rose pink	55cm	Aniseed scented
'Sunrise'	Canary yellow	75cm	Large flowered
tetragona	White	15cm	Fragrant
tetragona 'Johann Pring'	Deep pink	15cm	Large flowers
tuberosa	White	90cm	Vigorous
tuberosa 'Richardsonii'	White	75cm	Compact habit
'Virginalis'	White	55cm	Semi-double flowers

Flowering Bog Garden Plants
Plants for moist or wet situations beside the pool

NAME	COLOUR	FLOWERING TIME	HEIGHT	SPECIAL FEATURES
Aruncus sylvester	Creamy white	July-Aug.	1.5-2m	Spire-like growth
Astilbe chinensis 'Pumila'	Purplish rose	July	20-25cm	–
Astilbe crispa 'Lilliput'	Pink	July-Aug.	15cm	–
Astilbe crispa 'Perkeo'	Pink	July-Aug.	15cm	–
Astilbe 'Cattleya'	Lilac Pink	July-Aug.	75cm	Plumes of flowers
Astilbe 'Peach Blossom'	Soft Pink	July-Aug.	75cm	Plumes of flowers
Astilbe 'Red Sentinel'	Crimson	July-Aug.	75cm	Plumes of flowers
Astilbe 'White Gloria'	White	July-Aug.	75cm	Plumes of flowers
Cardamine pratensis	Lilac	April	30cm	–
Cardamine pratensis flore-plena	Lilac	April	30cm	Double blossoms
Filipendula hexapetala flore-plena	White	June-July	60cm	Delicate filigree foliage
Filipendula ulmaria 'Aurea'	Creamy white	June-July	75-100cm	Golden foliage
Filipendula ulmaria flore-plena	Creamy white	June-July	1m	Double blossoms
Iris aurea	Yellow	June	1m	–
Iris bulleyana	Blue	June	40cm	Grassy foliage
Iris kaempferi and varieties	Blue/pink/white	June	45-75cm	–
Iris ochroleuca	White and gold	June	1m	Handsome glaucous foliage
Iris setosa	Blue	June	25-30cm	Broad sword-shaped leaves
Iris setosa nana	Blue	June	15cm	–
Iris sibirica	Sky blue	June	75-90cm	–
Iris sibirica 'Blue Moon'	Blue	June	75-90cm	–
Iris sibirica 'Caesar'	Purple	June	75-90cm	–
Iris sibirica 'Emperor'	Deep violet blue	June	75-90cm	–
Iris sibirica 'Mrs Saunders'	Dark blue	June	75-90cm	–
Iris sibirica 'Perry's Pigmy'	Deep blue	June	35cm	–
Iris sibirica 'Snow Queen'	White	June	75-90cm	–
Lobelia cardinalis	Red	Aug.-Sept.	75-90cm	Bright green leaves
Lobelia fulgens	Red	Aug-Sept.	75-90cm	Beetroot coloured foliage
Lobelia syphilitica	Blue	Aug.-Sept.	60cm	–
Lobelia vedrariensis	Violet	Aug.-Sept.	1m	Foliage suffused with maroon
Lysimachia nummularia	Yellow	June-July	Prostrate	Useful scrambling habit
Lysimachia nummularia 'Aurea'	Yellow	June-July	Prostrate	Golden leaves
Lythrum 'Lady Sackville'	Rose pink	July-Sept.	75-100cm	Spire-like growth
Lythrum 'Robert'	Pink	July-Sept.	75-100cm	Spire-like growth
Lythrum salicaria	Rose purple	July-Sept.	1m	Spire-like growth
Lythrum 'The Beacon'	Rosy red	July-Sept.	75-100cm	Spire-like growth
Mimulus 'A.T. Johnson'	Yellow spotted maroon	May-July	25-40cm	–
Mimulus 'Bonfire'	Red	May-July & Sept.	25-35cm	–
Mimulus cardinalis	Red	July-Sept.	60cm	–
Mimulus 'Hose-In-Hose'	Yellow	May-July	25-35cm	One flower inside another
Mimulus lewisii	Lilac pink	July-Aug.	45-60cm	–
Mimulus 'Scarlet Emperor'	Red	May-July & Sept.	25-35cm	–
Mimulus 'Whitecroft Scarlet'	Scarlet	May-July	8cm	–
Mimulus 'Yellow Velvet'	Yellow freckled with maroon	May-July & Sept.	25-35cm	–
Peltiphyllum peltatum	Pink	April	45cm	Bronze-green foliage
Petasites fragrans	Lilac pink	Nov.-March	30-60cm	Fragrant flowers
Petasites japonicus	White	Feb.-March	1m	Immense leaves
Primula aurantiaca	Reddish orange	May-June	30cm	Candelabra type
Primula beesiana	Rose purple	May-June	45cm	Candelabra type
Primula bulleyana	Orange	May-June	45cm	Candelabra type
Primula burmanica	Rose purple	May-June	45cm	Candelabra type
Primula cockburniana	Orange scarlet	May-June	25-30cm	–
Primula denticulata	Blue-lilac	March-April	30cm	Drumstick-like flower heads
Primula denticulata alba	White	March-April	30cm	–
Primula denticulata cashmireana	Lilac purple	March-April	30cm	Leaves covered in a yellowish meal
Primula florindae	Sulphur yellow	May-June	60cm	Pendant blossoms

Flowering Bog Garden Plants (continued)

NAME	COLOUR	FLOWERING TIME	HEIGHT	SPECIAL FEATURES
Primula japonica	Purplish red	May-June	45cm	Candelabra variety
Primula japonica 'Miller's Crimson'	Crimson	May-June	45cm	Candelabra variety
Primula japonica 'Postford White'	White	May-June	45cm	Candelabra variety
Primula microdonta alpicola	Soft yellow	May-June	45cm	Mealy stems and leaves
Primula microdanta alpicola violacea	Deep mauve	May-June	45cm	Mealy stems and leaves
Primula pulverulenta	Magenta	May-June	45cm	Mealy stems
Primula pulverulenta 'Bartley Strain'	Buff/peach/pink	May-June	45cm	Mealy stems
Primula rosea and 'Delight'	Rose pink	March-April	15cm	—
Primula sieboldii	White/pink	May-June	30cm	Soft crimpled foliage
Primula sikkimensis	Soft yellow	May-June	30cm	Sweetly scented blossoms
Primula vialii	Red and lilac	May-June	30cm	Flower spikes like those of a red hot poker
Primula waltonii	Violet purple	May-June	35cm	Clustered flower head
Trollius 'Canary Bird'	Yellow	April-June	60-75cm	Globular blossoms
Trollius 'Fire Globe'	Deep orange	April-June	60-75cm	Globular blossoms
Trollius 'Orange Princess'	Orange	April-June	60-75cm	Globular blossoms
Zantedeschia aethiopica 'Crowborough'	White	June-Aug.	60-75cm	—

Bog Garden Ferns

NAME	HEIGHT	SPECIAL FEATURES
Dryopteris cristata	30cm	Pale green fronds, creeping habit
Matteuccia struthiopteris	1m	Bright green shuttlecocks
Onoclea sensibilis	45cm	Pinkish fronds turning green
Osmunda regalis	1-2m	Green fronds turning bronze in autumn
Osmunda regalis 'Cristata'	1m	Tassellated fronds
Osmunda regalis 'Purpurescens'	1-1.5m	Purplish fronds
Osmunda regalis 'Undulata'	1m	Crimpled and crested fronds
Dryopteris palustris	60-90cm	Finely cut fronds
Woodwardia virginica	45-75cm	Olive-green fronds

Foliage Bog Garden Ferns

NAME	HEIGHT	SPECIAL FEATURES
Gunnera manicata	2m	Immense coarse rhubarb-like foliage
Hosta 'Aurea'	30cm	Golden leaves age to green
Hosta fortunei	30-45cm	Bright green leaves
Hosta sieboldiana	45-60cm	Immense glaucous leaves
Hosta 'Thomas Hogg'	45cm	Green leaves edged white
Hosta undulata medio-variegata	30cm	Twisted cream and green foliage
Hosta ventricosa	70cm	Slightly wavy-edged leaves with bell-shaped, deep purple flowers
Rheum palmatum	up to 2m	Large green leaves
Rheum palmatum 'Bowles' Crimson	up to 2m	Purplish foliage
Rheum palmatum tanguticum	up to 2m	Purplish leaves, deeply cut

Marginal Plants

All the following marginal plants will grow with a varying degree of success between moist soil at water level and 20cm of water

NAME	COLOUR	FLOWERING TIME	HEIGHT	SPECIAL FEATURES
Acorus calamus	Green	June-July	90cm	Tangerine scented leaves
Acorus calamus 'Variegatus'	Green	June-July	75cm	Cream and green foliage
Acorus gramineus 'Variegatus'	Green	June-July	25cm	Cream and green foliage
Acorus pusillus 'Variegatus'	Green	June-July	25cm	Cream and green foliage
Alisma parviflora	Pink or white	June-Sept.	50-75cm	Rounded foliage
Alisma plantago-aquatica	Pink or white	June-Sept.	1m	Handsome ovate leaves
Butomus umbellatus	Pink	July-Sept.	50-75cm	Narrow triquetrous foliage
Calla palustris	White	April-June	20cm	Glossy foliage, red berries
Caltha leptosepala	White	March-May	40cm	Rich green leaves
Caltha leptosepala grandiflora	White	March-May	40cm	Immense blossoms
Caltha palustris	Yellow	March-May	30cm	Earliest flowered aquatic
Caltha palustris alba	White	March-May	30cm	–
Caltha palustris 'Flore Pleno'	Yellow	March-May	25cm	Double blossoms, compact habit
Caltha polypetala	Yellow	March-May	90cm	Immense stature
Carex pendula	Brownish green	May-July	60-90cm	Handsome broad green foliage
Carex riparia 'Bowles' Golden'	Brown	May-July	60cm	Golden foliage
Carex riparia 'Variegata'	Brown	May-July	60cm	Green and white variegated leaves
Cyperus longus	Greenish brown	May-July	60-90cm	Umbrella-like foliage
Cyperus vegetus	Reddish mahogany	May-July	60cm	Broad umbrella-like foliage
Eriophorum angustifolium	Greenish white	May-July	30-40cm	Fluffy white seeding heads
Eriophorum latifolium	Greenish white	May-July	30-40cm	Fluffy white seeding heads
Glyceria maxima variegata	Greenish white	June-July	60-90cm	Cream and green striped leaves
Houttuynia cordata	Creamy white	June-Aug.	30cm	Bluish green foliage
Houttuynia cordata 'Plena'	Creamy white	June-Aug.	30cm	Double blossoms
Hypericum elodes	Yellow	July-Sept.	8-15cm	Excellent scrambler for disguising pool edge
Iris laevigata	Blue	June	60-90cm	–
Iris laevigata 'Alba'	White	June	60-90cm	–
Iris laevigata 'Monstrosa'	Violet and white	June	60-90cm	–
Iris laevigata 'Rose Queen'	Pink	June	60-90cm	–
Iris laevigata 'Variegata'	Blue	June	60-90cm	Cream and green foliage
Iris pseudacorus bastardi	Primrose	June	75-90cm	–
Iris pseudacorus 'Golden Queen'	Yellow	June	75-90cm	–
Iris pseudacorus 'Variegata'	Yellow	June	75cm	Golden and green foliage
Iris versicolor	Violet and purple	June	60-75cm	–
Iris versicolor 'Kermesina'	Deep plum	June	60-75cm	–
Juncus effusus 'Spiralis'	Brown	June-July	35-45cm	Corkscrew-like foliage
Juncus effusus 'Vittatus'	Brown	June-July	35-45cm	Golden and green barred foliage
Lysichitum americanum	Yellow	April	30cm	Immense leaves
Lysichitum camtschatcense	White	April	30cm	Immense leaves
Mentha aquatica	Lilac pink	July-Sept.	30-45cm	Aromatic foliage
Menyanthes trifoliata	White or pinkish	April-May	20-30cm	Broad bean-like foliage
Mimulus ringens	Blue	June-Aug.	45cm	–
Myosotis scorpioides	Blue	May-July	20cm	Scrambling foliage
Peltandra alba	White	June-July	45cm	Arrow-shaped foliage
Peltandra virginica	Green	June-July	45-60cm	Arrow-shaped foliage
Preslia cervina	Blue	June-Aug.	30cm	Aromatic foliage
Ranunculus lingua	Yellow	May-June	60-90cm	Purplish-green foliage
Ranunculus lingua 'Grandiflora'	Yellow	May-June	60-90cm	Large flowers
Sagittaria japonica	White	July-Sept.	45-60cm	Arrow-shaped leaves
Sagittaria japonica 'Flore Pleno'	White	July-Sept.	45-60cm	Double flowers
Sagittaria latifolia	White	July-Sept.	1m	Arrow-shaped leaves
Sagittaria latifolia 'Flore Pleno'	White	July-Sept.	1m	Double flowers
Sagittaria sagittifolia	White	July-Sept.	45-60cm	Arrow-shaped foliage
Saururus cernuus	White	June-July	30cm	Red autumn foliage
Scirpus 'Albescens'	Reddish brown	July	60-90cm	Sulphureous-white foliage
Scirpus lacustris	Reddish brown	July	60-90cm	Spiky green leaves

Marginal Plants *(continued)*

NAME	COLOUR	FLOWERING TIME	HEIGHT	SPECIAL FEATURES
Scirpus tabernaemontani	Reddish brown	July	60-90cm	Spiky blue-green leaves
Scirpus tabernaemontani 'Zebrinus'	Reddish brown	July	60-75cm	Cream and green banded foliage
Typha laxmannii	Brown poker heads	Aug.-Sept.	1m	Slender willowy foliage
Typha minima	Brown poker heads	Aug.-Sept.	45cm	Grassy foliage
Veronica beccabunga	Blue	June-Sept.	15-20cm	Scrambling evergreen foliage

Deep Water Aquatics
Plants requiring similar conditions to waterlilies and with leaves that float on the surface of the water

NAME	COLOUR	FLOWERING TIME	DEPTH OF WATER	SPECIAL FEATURES
Aponogeton distachyus	White and black	April-Oct.	30-60cm	Vanilla scented flowers
Brasenia schreberi	Purple	June-July	30-60cm	–
Nuphar microphyllum	Yellow	June-Aug.	30-50cm	Translucent underwater foliage
Nuphar pumila	Yellow	June-Aug.	30-50cm	Translucent underwater foliage
Nymphoides peltata	Yellow	June-Sept.	30-60cm	–
Orontium aquaticum	White and yellow	April-May	up to 45cm	–

Floating Aquatic Plants
All the following floating plants will grow in any depth of water between 20-90cm

NAME	COLOUR	FLOWERING TIME	SPECIAL FEATURES
Azolla caroliniana	–	No flowers	Green or pinkish foliage
Azolla filiculoides	–	No flowers	Green or pinkish foliage
Eichhornia crassipes	Blue and lilac	June-Sept.	Handsome inflated foliage
Hydrocharis morsus-ranae	White	June-Aug.	Neat habit for miniature pools
Lemna trisulca	–	Insignificant flowers	Good green food for fish
Stratiotes aloides	White	June-Aug.	Spiny pineapple-like foliage
Trapa natans	White	June-Aug.	Handsome rhomboidal foliage
Ultricularia vulgaris	Yellow	Aug.-Sept.	Filigree foliage

Submerged Aquatic Plants
All submerged aquatic plants will tolerate water depths between 20-50cm. Most produce flowers, but apart from those noted, none are of any significance.

NAME	SPECIAL FEATURES
Callitriche hermaphroditica	Good green food plant for fish
Callitriche platycarpa	Good green food plant for fish
Ceratophyllum demersum	Grows in cool shady situations
Elodea canadensis	Vigorous grower
Eleocharis acicularis	Neat habit for miniature pools
Fontinalis antipyretica	Will tolerate moving water
Hottonia inflata	Inflated flower stems
Hottonia palustris	Lilac flowers in late spring
Isoetes lacustris	Evergreen foliage
Lagarosiphon major	Vigorous grower
Myriophyllum spicatum	Excellent spawning plant
Myriophyllum verticillatum	Excellent spawning plant
Potomogeton acutifolius	Bronze green translucent foliage
Potomogeton crispus	Bronze green crinkled translucent foliage
Ranunculus aquatilis	White and yellow flowers in midsummer
Tillaea recurva	Evergreen foliage

Definition of Terms

BRACT
A leaf in the axil of which a flower arises.

CAUDAL
Near the tail

CORDATE
Heart-shaped

CULTIVAR
A named cultivated variety of plant

DORSAL
Near or belonging to the back

EXCRESCENCE
An abnormal protuberance

FLACCID
Soft or flabby

GLAUCOUS
Sea-green, covered with a fine bloom

HIRSUTE
Hairy

INFLORESCENCE
The arrangement of a group of flowers

LANCEOLATE
Lance-shaped

ULM
Accumulated debris on the pool

OCTAPLOID
Having four times the basic chromosome number

ORBICULAR
Spherical

OVATE
Egg-shaped

PETALOID
Brightly coloured and resembling petals

PROCUMBENT
Lying loosely along the surface of the ground

PUBESCENT
Softly hairy

RACEME
An unbranched racemose inflorescence

RHOMBOIDAL
Roughly diamond-shaped

SAGITTATE
Arrow-shaped

SEPALS
Green and leaf-like outer series of perianth segments

SERRATED
Toothed like a saw

SPADIX
Fleshy spike-like flower head

SPATHE
Leaf-like sheath enveloping a spadix

STAMENS
Male reproductive organ in a flowering plant

STELLATE
Star-shaped

STOLONS
Shoot from a plant – runner or sucker

TRANSLUCENT
Semi-transparent

TRIFOLIATE
Three-lobed leaves

TRIPARTITE
Divided into three parts

TRIQUETROUS
Having three acute angles

TURBUCLE
Spherical or ovoid swelling

TURION
Detachable winter buds

UMBEL
A flower cluster in which the stalks arise from a common centre on the main stem

WHORL
A ring of leaves, flowers or petals

Index

Bold page numbers refer to Illustrations